Essentials of Exceptionality and Special Education

Neena Dash
M. Dash

ATLANTIC
PUBLISHERS & DISTRIBUTORS (P) LTD

Published by

ATLANTIC

PUBLISHERS & DISTRIBUTORS (P) LTD

7/22, Ansari Road, Darya Ganj,
New Delhi-110002
Phones : +91-11-23273880, 23275880, 23280451
Fax : +91-11-23285873
Web : www.atlanticbooks.com
E-mail : info@atlanticbooks.com

Branch Office
5, Nallathambi Street, Wallajah Road,
Chennai-600002
Phones : +91-44-64611085, 32413319
E-mail : chennai@atlanticbooks.com

Printed in India at Nice Printing Press, A-33/3A, Site-IV, Industrial Area, Sahibabad, Ghaziabad, U.P.

Preface

Teaching 'Exceptional' children has been a challenging job. This book *Essentials of Exceptionality and Special Education* provides varied and comprehensive study on this subject. Particular cases of exceptional children have been individually dealt with in the book providing the guidelines for the teachers for handling special cases.

The National Curriculum Framework for School Education (NCERT, 2000) emphasized, among other things, "preparing teachers with initial induction and sensitizing them through in-service education programmes to help them attend to the special needs of the learners with various challenges and equipping these teachers with skills, competencies, and strategies required to cater to the diversity in an inclusive setting." Thus, the book has been written to make up for this special need to train the students of B.Ed. and JBT courses in a way that they may efficiently manage the children with exceptionality.

This book has been designed as per the syllabi for B.Ed. students of M.D. University, Kurukshetra University and J.N. University although it may meet the needs of B.Ed. students of other Indian universities and JBT students as well.

In designing the contents of this book, great care has been taken to simplify complicated facts while at the same time latest trends and techniques have been incorporated in it. Exhaustive attempts have been made to pinpoint facts in simple and lucid language as far as possible.

We are extremely grateful to Er. Lalit Pathak, Managing Director of Krishma Educational Centre, Ner Chowk (Mandi) for giving us the permission to utilise the rich resources of his library and the computer facilities for preparing the manuscript of this book.

We convey our heartfelt thanks to all the authors and publishers whose publications have been of immense value to us in designing the contents of the book.

We express our sincere thanks to Dr. K.R. Gupta, Chairman of Atlantic Publishers and Distributors, New Delhi, for his prompt service and encouraging response in bringing out the book in time.

NEENA DASH
M. DASH

Contents

1

Exceptionality

1. MEANING OF EXCEPTIONALITY

At some time or other, practically all school teachers will have exceptional children in their classrooms. These children can become contributing members of the community. In a democratic country like ours every child has the right to education — the right to receive help in learning to the limits of his capacity, whether that capacity be small or great. It is consistent with a democratic philosophy that all children be given equal opportunity to learn whether they are exceptional or normal.

The term 'exceptional' means different things to different people. Some use it when referring to the particularly bright children or the child with unusual talents, others use it when they refer to any typical or deviant child. According to Telford and Sawrey (1972), "To be exceptional is to be rare or unusual."

Kirk (1962) defines an exceptional child as "that child who deviates from the average or normal child in mental, physical, or social characteristics to such an extent that he requires a modification of school practices, or special education services in order to develop to his maximum capacity."

Cruickshank (1974) also holds similar view when he defines an exceptional child as "a child who deviates intellectually, physically, socially, or emotionally so much from what is considered to be normal growth and development that he cannot receive maximum benefit from regular school programme and requires a special class or supplementary instruction and services."

Hewett and Forness (1984) have given a comprehensive definition of exceptional learner: "An exceptional learner is an individual who, because of uniqueness in sensory, physical, neurological, temperamental or intellectual capacity and/or in the nature and range of previous experience, requires an adaptation of the regular school programme in order to maximize his or her functioning level." The present authors accept this definition as all children traditionally leveled as exceptional fall under this definition.

2. NATURE OF EXCEPTIONALITY

An analysis of the definition given by Hewett and Forness (1984) reveals the following facts about the nature of exceptionality:

(i) Exceptionality refers to uniqueness. The uniqueness of the exceptional child may be noticed in one or more of the following dimensions — vision, hearing, movement, perceptual-motor, communication, social-emotional and intelligence. Thus, the blind, deaf, orthopaedically handicapped, learning disabled, speech handicapped, emotionally disturbed, socially disadvantaged, mentally retarded, slow learner and gifted are exceptional.

(ii) Exceptionality is related, in part, to the amount and quality of previous experiences received in the home.

(iii) The uniqueness of the exceptional child may be in the negative direction (as in case of handicapped children) or in the positive direction (as in case of gifted children).

(iv) Exceptionality is more quantitative than qualitative. A qualitative conception of exceptionality conceives of such children as constituting separate and, in many ways, distinct categories or classes of individuals. As separate categories of individuals, they are considered to have traits and characteristics which make them fundamentally different from the general run of mankind. They are supposed to learn, perceive, think, and adjust in ways which are unique to them; therefore they can not be understood in terms of principles which have been derived from and are applicable to normal individuals.

The trend of thinking over the last hundred years has been away from qualitative conceptions, and towards a quantitative frame of reference. The quantitative conception of exceptionality holds that the differences between the deviant groups and the normal are only differences of degree and not of kind. Thus the perceptual, conceptual, learning, and ideational processes of all individuals whether normal or exceptional are fundamentally the same. We all learn, retain, recall, perceive, think, and make personal and social adjustments according to the same general principles and patterns, but some of us do these things faster, better, more accurately, and more appropriately than others.

However, research findings on qualitative vs. quantitative nature of exceptionality are inconclusive at present. Hence, we have to wait for an answer to the question of whether the differences between the normal and the exceptional are qualitative or quantitative.

(v) Exceptionality has variable meanings in different social contexts. Social influences are undoubtedly responsible for some of the components of the patterning of traits characterizing the various categories of exceptional people. Deviations from the norm in the various ways labeled 'exceptional' may not, of themselves, result in characteristic personality and behavioral patterns, they do so because of the social or personal meanings attached to the deviations. Once a child is labeled as exceptional, society perceives him as different, labels him as different, treats him differently and expects him to act differently. The child, in turn, accepts these social judgments, perceives himself differently and act in accordance with these self-perceptions. "The argument is that, although the inherent differences between the normal and the various categories of exceptional people may be largely confined to the area of their exceptionality, these differences invariably spread to other areas as the result of social learning" (Teleford and Sawrey, 1972). Variations among individuals are universal, but society determines which deviations will be considered exceptional. Hence, the term "exceptionality" should always be understood in the particular social context in which it is used. This is more pragmatic.

(vi) Exceptionality has direction as well as intensity. Exceptional people differ in the mode of their exceptionality as well as in the degree of their deviation. The mode of exceptionality refers to the areas in which individuals deviate from the average which has been stated earlier. This is not to suggest that all exceptional individuals can be classified into discrete categories. In fact some exceptional people are exceptional in more than one area. For example, there are individuals who are both blind and deaf. Most individuals with cerebral palsy have speech, sensory, or intellectual defects in addition to their motor handicaps. It is also true that people who are handicapped in one way may excel in another. The crippled may be a genius or an artist.

The intensity of exceptionality refers to the degree of deviation. For example, in the intellectual dimension, some children are found to be extremely gifted, and some are found to be intellectually inferior. The intellectually inferior are usually broken down into several sub-groups — mildly retarded, moderately retarded and severely retarded. The degree or intensity of deviation may be as important as the facts of deviation. The intensity of exceptionality is just as important in the intellectual area as in the physical and other areas.

(vii) Exceptionality is also characterized by its extensity or breadth. Extensity is indicated by the degree to which the primary deviation affects other aspects of one's personality and behaviours. There is a belief that there is an inherent relationship between deviation in one area and corresponding behavioural and personality deviation in other areas. But such a belief is not supported by research findings. Even though there is no causal relationship between deviation in one area, and behaviour in other areas, research studies regularly find a greater incidence of social withdrawal, over-aggressiveness, personal unhappiness and all types of defensive behaviour patterns among individuals who deviate from the norm in ways culturally defined as undesirable than among individuals who are either closer to the group norm or who deviate in socially approved directions.

3. CONCEPTS OF IMPAIRMENT, DISABILITY AND HANDICAP

In past several terms have been used to describe exceptionality: insane, blind, deaf, crippled, feebleminded and so on. When the intellectually superior were included along with the intellectually inferior the term exceptional was adopted to refer to the entire group. Although the term 'exceptional' does not carry any connotation of inferiority or inadequacy, it is too non-specific to help us to understand children with disabilities. This has resulted in using terms like impaired, disabled, and handicapped. Although these three terms carry different meanings people started to use these three terms interchangeably. As a result of widespread debate, discussions and research, the World Health Organization (WHO, 1976) has clearly distinguished the use of three terms: Impairment, Disability and Handicap. These terms are based on an organic model having functional inter-relationship:

Impairment ⟶ Disability ⟶ Handicap

A discussion on these three terms is useful for the present purpose. "Impairment means abnormalities of body structure and appearance and organ or system function resulting from any cause in principle. Impairment represents disturbances at the organ level" (WHO, 1976). An impairment is a permanent abnormality. This may be so from birth, or acquired later. Example : a hole in the ear drum, a missing or defective part of the body, myopia, low level of intelligence, etc. Impairment may cause functional limitations. Functional limitation means partial or total inability to perform activities of which a human being is normally capable such as walking, lifting loads, seeing, hearing, speaking, reading, writing, etc. Impairment leads to disability.

"Disability reflects the consequences of impairment in terms of functional performance and activity by the individual" (WHO, 1976). Disability is defined as an existing difficulty in performing one or more activities which are generally accepted as essential components of daily living. Due to impairment there is a reduction in functional ability. For example, due to the hole in the ear drum, the child is unable to hear normally. A visually impaired child cannot see properly because of faulty image formation. Depending, in part, on the duration of functional limitation disability may be short-term, or long-term, or permanent.

Just as impairment leads to disability, disability handicaps the individual. "Handicap refers to disadvantages experienced by the individual as a result of impairments and disabilities. Handicaps thus reflect interaction with an adaptation to the individual's surroundings" (WHO, 1976). Handicap means a restriction imposed/acquired by the individual's disability which affects the efficiency of his/her day-to-day life activities. The term "handicap" refers to the problems a person with a disability or impairment encounters in interacting with the environment. A disability may pose a problem in one environment but not in another. For example, the child with an artificial limb may be handicapped when competing against non-disabled peers in a football match but experiences no problem in learning. Thus, a disabled child is not handicapped unless the disability leads to educational, personal, social, vocational, or other problems. The handicapping effects of a disability can be reduced by corrective services and medical interventions, etc.

4. TYPES OF EXCEPTIONAL CHILDREN

Exceptional children deviate from the normal children either in positive direction or in the negative direction. Thus there are positive exceptionals and negative exceptionals. Table 1.1 presents different types of exceptional children who deviate from the normal children either in positive direction or in the negative direction:

TABLE 1.1

Types of Exceptional Children

(-ve direction)	(+ve direction)
Visually Impaired (Blind and Low vision)	Gifted Children
Hearing Impaired (Deaf and Hard-of-Hearing)	Talented Children
Learning Disabled	Creative Children
Mentally Retarded (Intellectually Challenged)	
Orthopaedically Impaired	
Speech Handicapped	
Socially Disadvantaged	
Emotionally Disturbed	
Delinquent Children	

Children with Hearing Handicap

The hearing handicapped children are those children who have a damaged hearing mechanism and face difficulty in speech and language development. There is loss of hearing. The degree of hearing loss is less in some children while it is more severe in others. The hearing handicapped children may be hard-of-hearing or deaf.

The hard-of-hearing children are those children who have hearing loss but who can hear if spoken too loudly without a hearing aid. A hearing aid will enable them to hear better.

The deaf are those who can not hear even if spoken to very loudly. They require preparation in basic skills through special techniques before they are admitted in general schools. Hearing aids help them to become more functional.

Children with Visual Handicap

The visually handicapped children are those who have problems with vision. Some visually handicapped children can read large print and are functional in their environment whereas some have severe vision loss and can not be taught through visual methods. The visual loss is measured with the help of Snellen Chart. Depending upon the degree of loss they may be partially sighted or blind.

The partially sighted are those who require large print or magnified print materials. Their visual acuity (sharpness of visual image) is very low (20/70 in the better eye). This means that the child can see at 20 ft. distance what a normal child sees at 70 ft. distance. Their eye-sight may be weak due to short-sightedness, long-sightedness, astigmatism, glaucoma or muscle detachment.

The blind are those who need to be taught through Braille or through aural method. Their visual acuity (sharpness of visual image) may fall at 2/200.

Children with Mental Retardation

Mentally retarded children are those who have a lower level of intellectual functioning and have problems in social adaptability. There are various degrees of mental handicap. Consequently there are various categories of mentally handicapped children — the Educable Mentally Retarded (EMR), the Trainable Mentally Retarded (TMR) and the Custodial Mentally Retarded (CMR).

The educable mentally retarded are those who have minimum educational retardation in school subjects. Such children have problems of social adjustment, but are usually not recognised as mentally retarded at the pre-school level. They need repetition of instruction. The adaptive behaviours of such children should be observed carefully by the teachers so that they can be identified in the early stages.

The trainable mentally retarded can be trained in vocational areas. They are poor in adaptive behaviour and may need training in daily living skills at the initial levels.

The custodial mentally retarded need help in developing daily living skills. They can be educated in special institutions/ special classes. They are very poor in adaptive behaviour. They need constant care and attention.

Children with Learning Disability

These children are like other children in intellectual functioning. They are not mentally retarded, nor do they have visual or hearing problems. But they have problems in spelling, reading, writing, arithmetic, listening and comprehension. Their problem may be due to cerebral dysfunction/emotional/ behavioural disturbance, but it is not due to mental retardation, sensory handicap or instructional practices. Depending upon the degree of disability such children may be categorized into mild learning disabled and severe learning disabled.

Such children have a severe discrepancy between their achievement and intellectual ability. Such children may have the following specific problems:

Reading disability

Writing disability

Problems in comprehension and communication

Problems in numerical ability.

Children with Speech Handicap

Speech handicap refers to minor and major speech and language problems. There are children with mild language and speech disorders in our classrooms, and they often go unnoticed. While speaking and writing they tend to omit, distort, add or substitute words, phrases, letters of the alphabet etc. They stammer and are quiet or have long gaps in speaking full sentences. Their problems should be corrected before they start school. The major types of speech disorders are:

voice disorders,

articulation or pronunciation disorders, and

fluency disorders.

Children with Multiple Handicaps

Multiple handicap refers to more than one handicap in the child. A child may be blind and deaf, blind and orthopaedically handicapped, deaf and orthopaedically handicapped, mentally retarded and orthopaedically handicapped and so on. In case of multiple handicap, one handicap may be primary handicap and the other secondary or one handicap may be more severe than the other handicaps. It is, therefore, important to identify the primary handicap and take measures accordingly.

Children with Orthopaedic Handicap

Some children have orthopaedic handicap or locomotor handicap. Locomotor handicap refers to problems with the functioning of bones, joints and muscles. In some cases the problems are so severe that they require artificial limbs to compensate for their crippling conditions. In other cases they need wheel chair or crutches.

Children with Emotional Disturbance

Children with emotional disturbance are very often considered as problem children in the school. An emotionally disturbed child has certain inner tensions which create anxiety, frustration, fears and impulsive behaviour. Such a child may find excuses for his inner tensions in some physical difficulty. An emotionally disturbed child may attempt to solve the anxiety by behaving in a premature or childish way, becoming aggressive towards other people, or withdrawing himself to the world of fantasy.

Gifted Children

Gifted children are in some way superior in intellectual ability to other children of the same age. Gifted children are those who have demonstrated high ability (including high intelligence), high creativity and high task commitment — a high level of motivation and the ability to see a project through to its conclusion. A variety of terms have been used to describe individuals who are superior in some way such as 'talented', 'creative', 'genius', and 'precarious' (remarkably early development in particular areas like language, music, mathematical ability).

Children with Creative Talents

In a school teachers may come across a few students who have the ability to produce something new — a composition, a system of ideas or a material or a process which is essentially new or novel, and previously unknown to them. Such children behave differently. They are courageous in their convictions. They have independent thinking and adjustment. They become absorbed and preoccupied in what they are doing. They are curious. They take risks. They are flexible in their opinions. They are intellectually self-confident.

Socially Disadvantaged Children

Most teachers encounter a group of children in their classrooms who appear lifeless, incurious, and deceptively unintelligent. They show lack of interest, involvement, and motivation for academic success. They show general academic underachievement. The cumulative deficiencies in learning ultimately lead to their wastage and stagnation. These children are socially, economically, and educationally disadvantaged. School readiness programme in preschool centres, enriched experiences, and remedial instrucation are very useful for them.

Delinquent Children

In schools teachers come across some children who violate school norms. They are defiant of social standards. They are involved in antisocial activities or criminal activities which are punishable under law. If such children are in the age-group of 12 to 18, if their antisocial activities are serious in nature and occur very frequently they are considered as delinquents.

5. SOCIETY'S RESPONSE — EXCLUSION OR INTEGRATION

There have always been exceptional children, but society's response towards exceptional children has not always been the same. A historical perspective will help us to understand how the attitude and response of the society towards the less fortunate children have changed over the centuries — from rejection and exclusion to integration and inclusion.

(i) In the earliest primitive societies, disabled babies were rejected by their parents and were killed because they were considered to be imperfect. The guiding principle was "Nothing imperfect should be brought up."

(ii) During the Middle Ages, the threat to survival of disabled children decreased due to deep religious convictions. But the mentally ill were considered to be possessed by evil sprits or demons. Mental and physical abnormalities were considered to be the result of anger of God or the divine punishment for a sin. People used to please God through prayer or rituals to drive the spirit out from the disabled child.

(iii) In India, even at present, parents of disabled children feel guilty and sometimes take the blame for the child's impairments on themselves. Disabled children are considered to be useless and a burden for the family. In some cases, disabled infants are left at the gates of churches or temples, abandoned in institutions or left to live helplessly in the corner of a room. The fate of the disabled girl child is still worse.

(iv) In the later part of eighteenth century society's response towards disabled children changed — from rejection and guilt feeling to finding ways of educating such children. Educators and physicians came out with strong evidence in support of educability of deaf, blind, mentally and physically disabled children. Special schools were established in different parts of USA, UK and France including our own country. Thus, different societies started showing positive attitude towards the education of disabled children. But these children were excluded from the mainstream of regular schools till 1960. In fact, all children who were wheel-chair-bound, not toilet trained, or considered uneducable were excluded from common schools.

(v) Along with the establishment of special schools, special classes in common schools were also expanded in some cases. Special classes in common schools came about not for humanitarian reasons, but because such children were unwanted in the regular classrooms. In India, society's response to provide education to disabled children in excluded settings of special schools continued even after impendence in 1947 with NGOs assuming greater responsibilities.

(vi) In the later half of twentieth century various societies began to recognize the rights of disabled children for a free and appropriate education in the least restrictive environment of regular schools. This led to integrated education for disabled children. A number of international and national initiatives have contributed significantly for the change in society's response towards disabled children — from exclusion to integration.

(vii) The Indian Education Commission (1964-66) emphasized that education of handicapped children should be "an inseparable part of the general education system". The Ministry of Social Welfare, Govt. of India sponsored the Scheme of Integrated Education for Disabled Children in the year 1974. The United Nations declared 1981 as the International Year of Disabled Persons. "Full Participation with Equality" was the underlying theme of this programme. The National Policy of Education (1986) emphasized that "Wherever feasible, education of children with locomotor handicap and other handicaps will be common with that of others.... The objectives should be to integrate the physically and mentally handicapped with the general community, to prepare them for normal growth and to enable them to face life with courage and confidence."

The UN Standard Rules for Persons with Disabilities also categorically directed the Governments for educating disabled children in integrated settings of regular schools. As per the recommendations of Economic and Social Commission for Asia and the Pacific (1992) India pledged to promote the integration of children and adults with disabilities in formal and non-formal educational programmes. In DPEP and Sarva Siksha Abhiyan also emphasis has been placed on integrated education for disabled children.

The Persons With Disability Act (1995) of Govt. of India has made integration of students with disability a legal responsibility of the Government.

The PWD Act States

The appropriate Government and the local authorities shall ensure that every child with a disability has access to free education in an appropriate environment till he attains the age of 18 years (Article 26a), endeavour to promote the integration of students with disabilities in the normal schools (Article 26b).

The historical perspective presented above makes it very clear that society's response towards disabled children has rightly changed from exclusion to integration. Even then children with severe disabilities are still excluded from the mainstream of the regular school. Only mildly and moderately disabled children are integrated in the regular classrooms. Teachers need to change their attitude towards disabled children. Disabled children are to be accepted by teachers and peers as equal members of the school community. They need to appreciate diversity in the regular classrooms. Diversity should be viewed as a gift for ensuring teachers' professional efficiency, not as a problem for them.

2

Special Education

1. MEANING OF SPECIAL EDUCATION

Special education means specially designed instruction which meets the special educational and related needs of an exceptional child. It is distinguished from regular education by some unusual quality, something uncommon, noteworthy. It is something special — special materials, special training techniques, special equipment and special help and/or special facilities may be required for special categories of children having special needs. For example low vision children may require reading materials in large print. Hearing impaired children may require hearing aid, auditory training, lip reading etc. Mentally retarded children may need skill training. Related services, such as special transportation, medical and psychological assessment, physical and occupational therapy and counselling may be required if special education is to be effective.

Special education as teaching

We may look at special education in terms of *who*, *what*, *where* and *how*. *Who*? Special education is meant for exceptional children whose special needs or abilities necessitate an individualized programme of education. An inter-disciplinary team of professionals — special educators, regular classroom teachers, psychologists, speech therapists, physiotherapists, and specialist doctors bear the responsibility of helping disabled children maximize their capabilities. *What*? Special education is sometimes differentiated from regular education by its curriculum — that is, by what is taught. For example, teaching self-help skills or training in reading and writing Braille is an important part of curriculum for the blind in special education institutions which is not found in regular education. It is said that in regular education the school system dictates the curriculum, but in special education the child's individual needs dictate the curriculum. *Where*? Special education can sometimes be identified by where it takes place. Whereas regular education is provided in the regular classroom, special education may be provided in special class, resource room, special school or in residential school. *How*? Special education can be differentiated from regular education by the method used by teacher. One special educator may use sign language to communicate with students. Another special educator may use task analysis and skill training for mentally retarded children. Still another special educator may use multisensory approach and process training while teaching a learning disabled child.

Special education is a profession, a service with tools and techniques to meet the special needs of exceptional children. It is individually planned, systematically implemented, and carefully evaluated instruction to help exceptional learners achieve the greatest possible personal self-sufficiency and success in present and future environments.

2. OBJECTIVES OF SPECIAL EDUCATION

Special education has the same objectives as those of regular education — human resources development through providing appropriate education to children, national development, social reconstruction, civic development, vocational efficiency, etc. In addition to these objectives special education has certain special objectives such as the following:

(i) Early identification and assessment of special needs of handicapped children.

(ii) Early intervention to prevent a handicapping condition from becoming a serious one for remediation of learning problems and compensation by teaching the child new ways of doing things.

(iii) Parent counselling about prevention and remediation of defects, care and training of handicapped children in daily living skills, self-help skills, pre-academic skills and communication skills.

(iv) Community mobilization and awareness of problems of handicapped children and their education.

(v) Rehabilitation of the handicapped.

The National Policy of Education (1986/1992) clearly stipulates that:

"The objective should be (i) to integrate the physically and mentally handicapped with the general community as equal partners, (ii) to prepare them for normal growth and (iii) to enable them to face life with courage and confidence."

The following measures have been envisaged in the Programme of Action (NPE-1986) for attainment of these objectives:

(i) Wherever it is feasible, the education of children with motor handicaps and other mild handicaps will be common with that of others.

(ii) Special schools with hostels will be provided, as far as possible, at district headquarters, for severely handicapped children.

(iii) Adequate arrangements will be made to give vocational training to the disabled.

(iv) Teacher training programme will be reoriented, in particular for teachers of primary classes, to deal with special difficulties of handicapped children.

(v) Voluntary efforts for education of the disabled will be encouraged in every possible way.

3. SCOPE OF SPECIAL EDUCATION

The scope of special education is very wide. In fact the scope of special education is changing and widening with the new research findings coming up at international level.

(i) In terms of types of children with disabilities special education covers children with visual handicaps (blind and low vision children), hearing handicaps (deaf and hard-of-hearing children), mental retardation (mentally challenged children), learning disability (reading disability, writing disability and numerical disability), speech handicaps (auditory disorder, vocal disorder, stuttering, cleft palate, etc.), orthopaedic handicaps (spina bifida, poliomyelitis, muscular dystrophy, arthritis) and multiple handicaps. In some literature delinquent children, emotionally disturbed children and socially disadvantaged children are also covered under special education. Gifted and creative children are also covered under special education by some authorities.

(ii) In terms of degree of disability, special education covers mildly, moderately and severely handicapped children. Mildly and moderately handicapped children are usually included in regular schools, and severely handicapped children are included in special schools and residential schools. After the World Conference on Special Education Needs held in Spain (1994) and the enactment of PWD Act (1995) in India the trend has been changed. Now special education is proposed to be provided to all children irrespective of their degree of disability in inclusive schools.

(iii) The scope of special education includes identification of disabled children based on physical and behavioural characteristics, assessment of such children (medical, psychological and functional assessment), their care and rehabilitation.

(iv) Placement of disabled children in the appropriate setting forms an important part of the scope of special education. There are various placement settings such as:

Residential schools

Special schools

Special classes in regular schools

Part-time placement in regular class and part-time placement in the special class

Full-time placement in inclusive schools.

Placement of disabled children in a particular setting

depends upon the degree of disability, nature and extent of previous training and experiences of the disabled child and his special educational needs.

(v) The scope of special education includes various types of intervention measures such as, environmental, administrative, social and academic and various levels of intervention such as, preventive, remedial and compensatory efforts.

(vi) Various support services for children and teachers and allied services like medical check up and care also come under the scope of special education.

(vii) Provision of aids and equipments for meeting the needs of exceptional children — their procurement and development by teachers form an important aspect of special education.

4. SIGNIFICANCE OF SPECIAL EDUCATION

Exceptional children are those children who deviate from the normal children to such an extent that they can not benefit from the traditional education system or the regular education process. They require special education to maximize their potentialities. They require specially trained teachers, special aids and equipments and special teaching-learning strategies. This is possible only in special schools or if there is a modification in the regular education classes and if regular schools are adaptive to the needs and abilities of exceptional children.

Exceptional children have unique needs. For instance the blind needs education through braille, orientation about the immediate environment and mobility training. The deaf child needs training in speech reading, lip reading, etc. If is special education which can meet the unique needs of exceptional children.

Before the development of special education exceptional children, particularly the severely affected children, were rejected by the parents and the community. They were considered as burden for the society. They were left at the temple gates or in a corner of a village. But today educators have established the fact that given proper education and training exceptional children can become self-dependent and assets for the society, not a burden for it. They can contribute significantly for social welfare and international peace process.

The history of special education movement clearly shows the importance of early intervention through special education and care in the life of exceptional children. Hellen Keller was born blind and deaf. The former American President, Roosevelt was handicapped by Polio. The sister of John F. Kennedy, a former American President was mentally retarded. Albert Einstein, the famous scientist was considered as a learning disabled child during his primary grades. The famous poets Bhima Bhoi and Surdas were blind by birth. They were able to compensate their disabilities by special education which started very early in their lives.

Education is a human right issue. Every child, whether he is disabled or non-disabled has right to education in an appropriate setting. Special education should be provided to disabled children either in inclusive setting of regular schools or in the segregated setting of special schools so that they can acquire the knowledge, competencies and skills which are essential to live as competent and contributing citizens in a Nation.

In past attempts to universalize elementary education failed because disabled children who constitute nearly 10 per cent of the total population of children in the age-group of 6-14 were ignored. Adequate measures were not taken to provide quality education to such children. Even today Sarva Siksha Abhiyan is in the focus in all the States and Union Territories of our country. The goals of Sarva Siksha Abhiyan can only be achieved if we provide special education to disabled children.

5. LEVELS OF INTERVENTION

Special education is an intervention designed to eliminate or, at least reduce, the obstacles that might keep a child from full and active participation in school and society. There are three levels of intervention efforts such as:

Preventive Efforts,

Remedial Efforts and

Compensatory Efforts.

Preventive Efforts

Preventive efforts are based on the notion that prevention is better than cure. Preventive efforts in special education aim at keeping possible problems from becoming a serious handicap. For example a low vision child has problem of seeing things or reading what is written on the black board clearly. As a preventive measure, the classroom should have adequate illumination. Similarly, a hard-of-hearing child has difficulty in listening to what the teacher says. Seating arrangement for such a child should be made in such a way that his better ear is directed towards the teacher. A wheel-chair-bound child has difficulty in climbing the staircase. He has problem of movement. As a preventive measure, architectural barriers should be removed from the school. The problems of a delinquent child who is rejected by his peers in the school or unwanted by parents in the home can be reduced by love, affection and care of the teacher. It is not enough for teachers to say "We love you". Love, affection and care of teachers should be reflected in their attitude and behaviour towards the delinquent child.

Remedial Programmes

Remedial programmes constitute the second level of intervention. Remedial programmes aim at helping the child to overcome his disability through training or education in special schools, special class or resource room in the regular school. This is particularly useful for those disabled children who had very little or no previous training in the home. For example, a deaf child has problem of understanding speech. For such a child training in lip reading, speech reading and use of residual hearing is useful for overcoming his disability. A blind child has difficulty in reading and writing. Such a child can be trained in Braille reading and Braille writing. Mobility training and orientation training are essential for blind children to overcome their disability to understand the environment and their problem of movement in and around the environment. Training in daily living skills are useful for mentally challenged children.

Compensatory Efforts

Compensatory efforts constitute the third level of intervention. This level of intervention aims at giving the child new ways to deal with the disability. Disability handicaps the child to function effectively in the school and the society. He needs compensatory aids and equipments to proceed satisfactorily according to his abilities and interest. For example, a low vision child needs to read large-print materials and use magnifying glass. A blind child needs Braille writer and Braille materials to compensate for his loss of vision. A hearing impaired child needs to use hearing aid (single cord or V cord) regularly to compensate for his loss of hearing. Such children can benefit more from visual cues during classroom instruction. Similarly, multi-sensory materials can bombard the senses of learning disabled children. Compensatory efforts for orthopaedically handicapped children constitute providing such children with crutches/wheel chairs and thick pens depending upon their specific impairment.

In fact these three levels of intervention are not distinct levels. In other words, these three levels of intervention should not occur one after the other. Rather these three levels should be introduced simultaneously so as to help the disabled child learn the academic skills, grow as independent and competent citizens and make satisfactory adjustment in the school and the society.

6. TYPES OF SPECIAL EDUCATION SERVICES

The type of special education services available for disabled children can be structured along a continuum that ranges from integration to segregation or full-time placement of disabled children in the regular classroom to twenty four hour institutional care. The type of services required depends primarily on the degree of disability and the nature of special needs. Seriously and profoundly handicapped children usually require more continuous, prolonged, and intensive care in special institutions. The following are various services available for handicapped children:

(i) *Full-time placement in a regular classroom.*

The least intensive level of special education service is placement of the disabled child in a regular classroom. The regular classroom teacher is provided with materials, equipment and instructional methods that are appropriate to the disabled child. At this level, the direct services of experts may not be required. The expertise of the regular classroom teacher may be sufficient to meet the child's needs. Usually speech handicapped, mildly mentally retarded, learning disabled, orthopaedically handicapped, visually impaired children who can work independently with Braille materials and the hard-of-hearing children can be full-time students in regular classroom.

(ii) *Full-time placement in a regular classroom with special education consultations.*

At the next level, the disabled child is a full time student in a regular classroom. The regular teacher has special materials and equipment to teach the disabled child. But he may need consultation with the special educator. The special educator instructs the regular teacher for selection and use of special materials, equipment and methods.

(iii) *Full-time placement in a regular classroom with provision of itinerant special educator service.*

Going a step further, the disabled child is a full-time student in a regular classroom. But he gets the services of an itinerant teacher. The itinerant teacher moves from school to school on a planned schedule and work directly with disabled children either individually or in small groups. He provides specialised instruction to the disabled child once or twice in a week and advises the regular teacher in the use of materials, equipment and methods. This plan can be used in rural areas where schools are far apart and too small to have full-time resource teachers.

(iv) *Full-time placement in a regular classroom with provision of a resource room/resource teacher.*

At the next level, the disabled child is enrolled in the regular classroom. But he receives specialised instruction from a resource teacher in the resource room. The length and frequency of such help depend on the severity of his problems. The resource teacher provides such instruction in the special classroom. The child returns to the regular classroom and participates in the regular classroom activities in music, art and physical education in the second half of the day.

(v) *Part-time placement in regular classroom with part-time placement in a special class.*

In this type of service the disabled child is a member of a special classroom. In view of his moderate disability and special needs he receives specialised instruction in academic subjects in a special classroom of the school for a half-day. The resource teacher provides such instruction in the special classroom. The child returns to the regular classroom and participates in regular classroom activities in music, art and physical education in the second half of the day.

(vi) *Full-time placement in a special class.*

This is the type of service usually provided to severely retarded children. This is also the oldest and traditional type of service for disabled children which has been criticized for it segregates disabled children from their normal peers. In this plan a group of ten to fifteen disabled children belonging to one particular category of disability are enrolled in a special class. Thus all MR children attend one special class. All hearing impaired children attend one special class. These children spend the whole day with the resource teacher in the special classroom being segregated from their normal peers in the school, except during recess, lunch, after school activities and school functions. In rural areas, where ten to fifteen children having same type of handicap are not available, children having different types of disability may be enrolled in a special class. But considerable demands are made on a teacher working with children with diverse problems.

(vii) *Full-time placement in special schools.*

Special schools provide an all day, segregated experience for disabled children. The special school is usually organized for a specific category of disabled children. It contains special equipment necessary for their care and education. The children return to their home after the school hour. There are special schools for blind, deaf and mentally retarded children in our country.

(viii) *Full-time placement in a residential school.*

The most restrictive type of services are usually provided in boarding or residential schools. This type of service is usually provided to blind, totally deaf, and profoundly retarded children. In this arrangement disabled children receive twenty-four hour care in the boarding school. They are isolated from their parents, siblings and the community. But they can visit their homes during vacation and on weekends. In residential schools children receive academic instruction in addition to training in social skills, communication skills, self-help skills, etc.

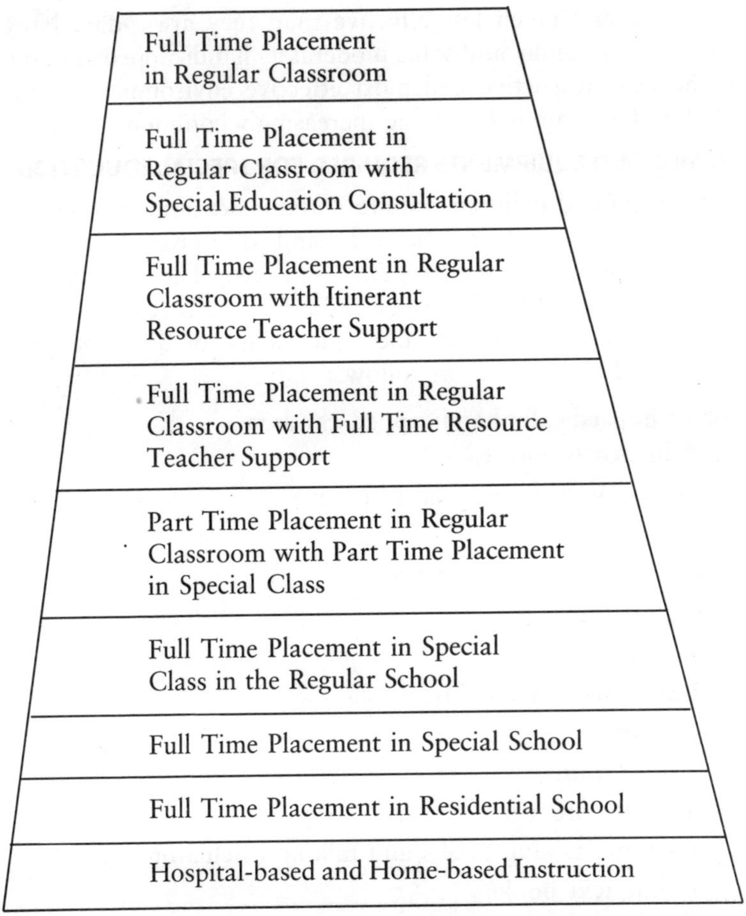

Continuum of Special Education Services

(ix) *Hospital and home-bound instruction.*

This involves teaching the handicapped children in the hospital or at home because of their physical and/or psychological conditions. This type of service is most often required for physically handicapped or emotionally disturbed children when no alternative is readily available. Typically, the child is confined to the hospital or his home for a relatively short period of time and the hospital or home-bound teacher maintains contact with the child's regular teacher.

Special education services in the past were much more restrictive and much less effective than they are today. Now placement of mildly and some moderately handicapped children in the least restrictive and most effective environment of the regular classroom is becoming increasingly common.

7. AIDS AND EQUIPMENTS REQUIRED FOR SPECIAL EDUCATION

Exceptional children require certain aids and equipments to compensate for their deficiencies and to receive education in special schools and/or regular schools. These aids and equipments which exceptional children require depend upon their uniqueness. The aids and equipments for different types of disabled children are as follows:

For orthopaedically handicapped children

- Adjusted furniture
- Special writing material (thick pen)
- Artificial limbs
- Wheel chairs and crutches

For blind children

- Brailler
- Braille slate and stylus, Braille sheets
- Abacus
- Taylor frame
- Tape Recorder
- Cassette, talking books and talking calculator
- Braille text books
- Bulletin board

Flat desks

Embossed graph sheets with rubber band and push pin tactile maps

Concrete objects to teach shape, size, thickness, weight, ascending and descending, etc. number, texture and motor coordination.

For hearing impaired children

Hearing aid (group hearing aid and individual hearing aid)

Speech trainer or voice trainer.

Picture albums

Mirror (big and small)

Special learning materials like flash cards, educational games and toy materials, handouts of classroom instruction.

For mentally retarded and learning disabled children

Educational games and play materials

Concrete objects for teaching different concepts

Picture cards and pictures

Day, Date and Month Calendar

Tool box

Aids for sensory-motor coordination

Alternate learning materials (simplified).

3

Mental Retardation

1. MEANING AND DEFINITION

In our society we have people with different mental abilities — average, more than average, and less than average. People with less than average mental ability are commonly called mentally retarded. Mentally retarded children were previously called idiots, feeble minded, moron, imbecile, etc. Now mentally retarded children are called mentally challenged or intellectually challenged. Similarly, the old terms like mental handicap, mental deficiency, and mental subnormality are now replaced by the term mental retardation.

There are many definitions of mental retardation. The most comprehensive among them is the one given by the American Association on Mental Retardation (AAMR). The definition as given in 1983 is:

"Mental Retardation refers to significantly sub-average general intellectual functioning, resulting in or associated with concurrent impairments in adaptive behaviour, and manifested during the developmental period."

Let us define the key terms in the definition cited above:

(i) 'General Intellectual Functioning' is defined as the result obtained by the administration of standardized general intelligence tests developed for the purpose, and adapted to the conditions of the region/country.

(ii) 'Significantly Subaverage' is defined as IQ of 70 or below on standardized measures of intelligence. The upper limit is intended as a guideline; it could be extended to 75 or more, depending upon the reliability of intelligence test used.

(iii) 'Adaptive Behaviour' is defined as the degree with which the individual meets the standards of personal independence and social responsibility expected of his age and cultural group. The expectations of adaptive behaviour may be reflected in the following areas:

- *During infancy and early childhood in*
  Sensory and motor skill development.
  Communication skills (including speech and language).
  Self help skills.
  Socialization.
- *During childhood and adolescence in*
  Application of basic academic skills to daily life activities.
  Application of appropriate reasoning and judgment in the mastery of the environment.
  Social skill.
- *During late adolescence and adult life in*
  Vocational and social responsibilities and performances.

(iv) 'Developmental Period' is defined as the period of time between conception and the 18th birthday.

New Definition of MR (AAMR-1992)

"Mental retardation refers to substantial limitation in present functioning. It is characterized by significantly subaverage intellectual functioning, existing concurrently and with related limitations in two or more of the following applicable adaptive areas: communication, self-care, home living, social skills, community use, self-direction, health and safety, functional academics, leisure and work. Mental retardation manifests before age 18."

Before labeling a person as mentally retarded especially in the mild category certain factors have to be considered. Members belonging to low socio-economic group and certain cultures may score low on standard tests of intelligence and thus may be labeled as mentally retarded. However, they will be functioning within normal limits according to their culture's criteria. Therefore, one must be cautious before labeling a person as mentally retarded.

Adaptive behaviour is given much more emphasis in determining whether or not a person is retarded. Thus, a child can score low on a test of intelligence but have adaptive skills. A child may do poorly in school but still be able to cope with the rural life, with peers, and after school job. Some children may function in the retarded range while they are in school for six hours of the day but behave normally once they return to the home community for the rest eighteen hours.

A child should not be labeled as mentally retarded simply because he scores low on intelligence test or because he has deficits in adaptive behaviour. A child is to be regarded as mentally retarded only when all the three conditions are noticed in him:

(i) Significantly subaverage intellectual functioning;
(ii) Deficits in adaptive behaviour and
(iii) The first two conditions are observed during the developmental period.

2. LEVELS OF SEVERITY

Mentally retarded children are classified in three different ways: medical, psychological and educational. The medical classification is based on the cause of retardation. The psychological classification is based on the levels of severity of retardation. It was originally recommended by the American Association of Mental Deficiency. The psychological classification is now used in special schools in India. The educational classification was originally recommended by American educators. It is based on the educability of retarded children. This classification has been recommended by National Council of Educational Research and Training (NCERT), New Delhi for use in IED units in regular schools.

In terms of levels of severity mentally retarded children are classified into mild, moderate, severe, and profound.

In other words, there are four levels of retardation: Mild Level, Moderate Level, Severe Level ppand Profound Level depending on the IQ ranges. table 3.1 presents the IQ ranges at different levels of retardation:

TABLE 3.1

Levels of Retardation

Levels of Retardation	IQ Ranges
Mild Retardation	IQ 55 to 70
Moderate Retardation	IQ 40 to 54
Severe Retardation	IQ 25 to 39
Profound Retardation	IQ below 25

The National Institute of Mentally Handicapped (Govt. of India) fixes the IQ ranges as follows:

Mild Level – IQ 50-70
Moderate Level – IQ 35-49
Severe Level – IQ 20-34
Profound Level – IQ below 20

In terms of educability, MR children are classified as Educable, Trainable and Custodial. The IQ ranges of these three types of MR children are given in table 3.2.

TABLE 3.2

Educational Classification of MR

Types of MR	IQ Ranges
Educable Mentally Retarded (EMR)	IQ 50 to 75
Trainable Mentally Retarded (TMR)	IQ 25 to 50
Custodial Mentally Retarded (CMR)	IQ below 25

The educable mentally retarded children are those who can be taught the basic academic subjects. The trainable mentally retarded are those children who can be taught functional academics with emphasis on self-help and vocational skills.

The custodial mentally retarded are those children who require constant and special care specially in a residential institution. The educable mentally retarded children, the mildly retarded and some moderately children having IQ 50 and above can be integrated in the general schools.

TABLE 3.3

Two Systems of Classification of MR Children

System \ IQ	100 95 90 85 80 75 70 65 60 55 50 45 40 35 30 25 20 15 10 5			
Psycho-logical	Mild	Moderate	Severe	Profound
Educa-tional	Educable	Trainable	Custodial	

The specific characteristics of MR Children at different levels of severity are given in table 3.4.

3. SYMPTOMS OF MR

Mentally retarded children show certain symptoms which may be physical and/or behavioural in nature. But these symptoms are not universally noticed among all retarded children, particularly the physical symptoms vary depending upon the severity of retardation. Some retarded children go unnoticed in the home and the school because they do not show external symptoms of retardation. For example, the mildly retarded or the educable mentally retarded remain unnoticed for a long time.

Physical Symptoms of Retardation

(i) A small or a big head

(ii) Big or small and slanting eyes

(iii) A thick tongue

(iv) Drolling of saliva

(v) Irregular teeth

(vi) Short and fat limbs

(vii) Flat feet

TABLE 3.4

Specific Characteristics of MR children at Different Severity Levels/Ages

Severity level/ Description	Mild	Moderate	Severe	Profound
Pre-schools 0-5 years	Can develop social and communication skills; minimal retardation in sensory motor areas; often not distinguished from normal until late age.	Can talk or learn to communicate; poor social awareness; fair motor development; profits from training in self help; can be managed with moderate supervision.	Poor motor development; speech minimal; generally unable to profit from training in self-help; little or no communication skills.	Gross retardation; minimal capacity for functioning in sensory motor areas; needs nursing care.
School age 6-20 years Training and Education	Can learn academic skills up to approximately 6th grade level by late teens; can be guided towards social conformity.	Can profit from training in social and occupational skills; unlikely to progress beyond 2nd grade level in academic subject; may learn to travel alone in familiar places.	Can talk or learn to communicate; can be trained in elementary health habits; profits from systematic habit training.	some motor development present; may respond to minimal or limited training in self-help.
Adult 21 and over Social and Vocational Adequacy	Can usually achieve social and vocational skills adequate to minimum self-support but needs assistance when under unusual social or economic stress.	May achieve self-maintenance in unskilled or semiskilled work under sheltered conditions; needs supervision and guidance when under mild social or economic stress.	May contribute partially to self-maintenance under complete supervision; can develop self-protection skills to a minimal useful level in controlled environment.	Some motor and speech development; may achieve very limited self-care; needs nursing care.

Behavioural Symptoms of Retardation:

(i) Delay in sitting, standing or walking
(ii) Cannot do things for himself such as eating, dressing, bathing and grooming
(iii) Speech not clear
(iv) Cannot understand instruction
(v) Difficulty in walking or moving the arms due to weakness and/or stiffness in the limbs
(vi) Occasional fits, rigidity or loss of consciousness
(vii) Backward, dull or slow in reaction
(viii) Cannot learn things like other children of his age
(ix) Cannot tell his name
(x) Lacks toilet control.

If the child shows the above physical symptoms and some of the behavioural symptoms mental retardation can be suspected.

4. CAUSES OF MENTAL RETARDATION

Research has indicated that mental retardation is largely inherited. It is organic in nature. But non-organic or environmental factors also cause mental retardation.

Organic Factors

The organic factors may be of pre-natal origin or perinatal origin.

(i) Pre-natal Factors:
- Cerebral mal-developments
- Chromosomal deviations
- Placental dysfunction
- Intra-uterine infections
- Teratogenes (malformation of genes)
- Diabetes of the mother
- Malnutrition of the pregnant mother
- Multiple pregnancies

(ii) Perinatal Factors:
- Complications of prematurity

- Birth trauma
- Suffocation of the baby-to-be born due to lack of oxygen at the time of birth
- Infections during the birth process

(iii) Post-natal Factors:

- Cerebro Vascular accident
- Neurotoxins
- Intra cranial infections
- Anoxic episodes
- Rabies
- Slow virus infections
- Defects in protein metabolism, Carbohydrate metabolism and fat metabolism
- Hormonal imbalance (thyroxin deficiency)
- Nutritional deficiencies

Environmental Factors

Environmental factors refer to those factors not in the chromosomes or genes of the parents but in their surroundings that affect the baby's brain. Examples — Illness of a mother during pregnancy, alcohol/drugs consumed by a mother during pregnancy; complicated delivery. These factors could affect the foetus'/baby's brain causing mental retardation.

Environmental factors affect the baby's brain before birth (during pregnancy), during birth and after birth (during childhood). And so for better understanding, we divide them into three situations —

1. Prenatal period (during pregnancy)
2. Natal period (during birth)
3. Postnatal period (after birth)

(i) *During pregnancy*

Infections/illnesses of the mother like anemia (paleness with weakness and tiredness)

Diabetes

Heart disease (palpitations/breathlessness)

High blood pressure (swelling of hands/feet with headache and giddiness)

Malaria

Measles (fever with rash)

Mumps

Sexually transmitted diseases

Tuberculosis (TB)

Exposure to X-Rays

Excessive consumption of alcohol/tobacco/cigarettes/pan

Intake of drugs/medicine

Attempted abortion by drugs or by an unqualified person

Accident/injury

Poor diet

Emotional trauma

(ii) *During birth*

Premature/prolonged labour

Complicated/instrumental delivery

Shortage of oxygen to the brain

Rh incompatibility

(iii) *After birth*

High fever

Convulsion (fits)

Viral infections like meningitis and encephalitis

Prolonged diarrhea

Jaundice/typhoid/tuberculosis

Accidents/head injuries

Lead/mercury poisoning

Poor diet

Lack of or partial immunization

Inadequate environmental stimulation.

5. PREVENTION OF MENTAL RETARDATION

Prevention of mental retardation can be at three levels:

Primary Level

Secondary Level and

Tertiary Level

(1) Primary Level Prevention

The purpose of prevention at primary level is to eliminate or reduce the occurrence and prevalence of mental retardation in the community. This can be done through the following ways:

Pre-natal Care — It aims at preventing pre-mature birth and low birth weight which are causative factors of mental retardation. It will guard the foetus against damage from maternal illness and infections. The pregnant mother should be advised to —

- have regular medical check up for early detection of abnormalities, illness and infections and treatment
- have good nutrition in the diet
- examine her blood and urine
- get immunization at appropriate time
- avoid unnecessary and non-prescribed drugs
- avoid physical accidents
- not to take alcohol, tobacco and poisonous substances
- avoid exposure to infections such as measles, rubella and syphilis
- avoid abortion in unskilled hands
- avoid mental tension

Perinatal Care — Good perinatal care is an important factor to prevent mental retardation.

- The pregnant mother should be advised to get delivery conducted by a trained personnel at home or at a health centre.
- For all complicated pregnancies and labours the delivery should be conducted at hospitals in order to bring

down injury and infection which are the causative factors of mental retardation in the child.

- All high risk infants should be well taken care of and should have a long term follow-up for early detection of handicapping conditions and delays in development.
- Early identification and prompt and appropriate treatment of infections can lessen the complications.
- Proper environmental and personal hygiene, clean water supply, destruction of insects and animals which carry infections will help to reduce the occurrence of infections and thereby the occurrence of mental retardation.
- The mother and the baby should be given good nutrition.

(2) Secondary Level Prevention

Secondary level prevention involves early identification of problems followed by early intervention which eliminates the potential factor or modify it so that mental retardation is prevented. This includes —

- Early treatment of protein deficiency and hormonal imbalance in the body.
- Blood and urine examination in the new born baby and immediate treatment in positive cases.
- Counselling to parents regarding mode of inheritance and risk factors in order to avoid further occurrence of mental retardation due to these factors.
- High risk infants care and follow up (premature birth, low birth weight cases).
- Early stimulation and intervention programmes for developmental delays through enriched environment and teaching for better parenthood.

(3) Tertiary Level Prevention

This aims at minimizing the long term disability or at least mitigating some of its effects. This involves specific or comprehensive services for individuals such as —

- Active immunization programmes to prevent infections like Diphtheria, Tetanus, Whooping Cough, Typhoid, Measles, Polio and Rubella

- Public awareness programmes about the causes, symptoms, preventions and treatment of mental retardation
- Awareness about family planning with reference to age of marriage, age of the mother to give birth to a child (between 20 to 35 year), spacing, limiting the size of the family, etc.
- Further research on prevention of mental retardation and developmental delays.

6. TREATMENT AND SERVICES FOR MENTAL RETARDATION

Mentally retarded children are like any other children excepting their retarded intellectual development. In view of their delayed development they need adequate care, proper services and treatment to avoid hazards of daily life.

(i) MR children should be provided three different types of services: health services, education and training, and rehabilitation services. Health services include regular medical check up by doctors and nurses and treatment of illness, if any. Education and training should cover daily living skills, self-help skills, basic academic subjects and adaptive behaviour. Rehabilitation services include vocational training in simple crafts and unskilled jobs.

(ii) Multi-disciplinary approach is the ideal approach to provide treatment and services for MR children. In developed countries, a team of specialists — psychologists, psychiatrists, physiotherapists, doctors, rehabilitation personnel, social worker and special educators — is at the service of MR children depending upon their degree of retardation. In our country this may not be feasible in all areas, particularly in rural areas. But social workers, NGOs, rehabilitation officers and special teachers can provide humanitarian services to MR children.

(iii) Treatment and services for MR children should start at an early age so that further damage to these children can be avoided.

(iv) Services to MR children can be provided at different levels:

- in hospitals where severely and profoundly retarded children can be taken care of by doctors and nurses;
- in day-care centres where MR children remain for the whole day in the custody of a care-taker and parents take back their children to the home in the afternoon. This type of service is advisable for working parents;
- in residential institutions where MR children remain day and night in the institution in the custody of school personnel. Parents can meet their children on week ends or take their children to the home during holidays.

(v) The most effective services is the home-based service. MR children require individual attention, lot of care, affectionate mother and secure environment. They are to be accepted by parents as equal members of the family. The most important thing is the attitude of parents towards their retarded children. Parents should not make any discrimination between their retarded child and other normal children in the family. Experienced mothers, grandmothers and other old women in the family are familiar with normal milestones of development. If a child is found to have delayed development and if abnormalities are noticed in his physical and intellectual development and if deficiencies are noticed in his adaptive behaviour he should be referred to paediatricians and child psychologists for diagnosis and treatment.

(vi) Parents should not feel dejected and disappointed about the condition of their children. They should not loose patience but instead should take all possible steps to prevent further damage through proper care and training as per the advice of doctors, psychologists and teachers.

(vii) Home-based training is most effective and provides the foundation for later learning in the school. Parents and particularly the mother should create conditions and teach the child daily living skills, social skills, communication skills and pre-academic skills during the first few years under reinforced practice and through enjoyable activities. Listening skills, attending skills, naming objects, manipulating objects, awareness of self, responding to and greeting others, conversation, reading pictures, music, play, games and story telling should be emphasized in the home-based training programme.

7. MANAGEMENT AND EDUCATION OF MENTALLY RETARDED CHILDREN

Management and education of MR children pose a challenge for educators. As per existing practice severely retarded children are educated in residential schools. Moderately retarded children are educated in special schools. As per the provisions contained in the centrally sponsored scheme of IEDC, mildly retarded or the educable mentally retarded children are to be educated in common with non-disabled children in the regular schools. But before mildly retarded or educable mentally retarded children are enrolled in regular schools it would be advisable to provide pre-school education to such children. In this section management and education of educable mentally retarded (EMR) children in regular schools are discussed.

Pre-School Education

Educable mentally retarded children in the age group of 3 to 6 years should be given pre-school education. During this period emphasis should be on developing readiness skills which are prerequisites for later learning of academics. Readiness skills are also recommended for normal youngsters. But pre-school classes for the mildly retarded child should start at a lower level and the training of these skills may take as long as two or three years rather than one year. Readiness skills include the ability to:

(i) Sit still and attend to the teacher.

(ii) Discriminate auditory and visual stimuli.

(iii) Follow directions.

(iv) Develop language.

(v) Increase gross and fine motor coordination (e.g. holding a pencil, cutting with a pair of scissors).

(vi) Develop self-help skills (e.g. tying shoes, buttoning and unbuttoning, zipping and unzipping, toileting).

(viii) Interact with peers in group situations. In short pre-school education should be a continuation of home-based training with re-emphasis on teaching sensori-motor skills, communication skills, social skills, daily living or self-help skills and pre-academic skills. The nature of training in pre-school classes depends on the degree of retardation, special needs and deficiencies in the child and the quality of home training received by the child.

Education in General School

(i) EMR children should receive education in common with others in general schools. Educational programme for the EMR children should aim at development of (a) Academic skills, (b) Social competence, (c) Personal adjustment and (d) Occupational adequacy.

(ii) Depending upon the nature of retardation they may be educated in the regular classroom or regular classroom with part time instruction in the resource room or special class in the regular school.

(iii) The curriculum at the primary stage should be an extension of that of pre-school education. The curriculum for EMR children should be oriented towards providing readiness skills, language development, concept formation, socially adaptive behaviours and teaching basics of reading, mathematics and handwriting. Teaching of tool subjects such as reading, arithmetic, handwriting, and oral language should be very simple and interesting and of the standard expected of normal kindergarten-age children.

(iv) If some retarded children are in need of special class instruction the following principles should be followed:

- The younger the children, the smaller the class.
- The more heterogenous the group, the smaller the class.
- Special class should always be organized within the regular primary school.

- Special class instruction should be given by the resource teacher or the itinerant teacher only.
- Adequate diagnosis should be made before they are placed in the special class.
- The resource teacher should have considerable freedom in adapting the curriculum to the needs of individual children.
- Whether the retarded child is educated in the regular classroom or resource room, instruction should be systematic and sequential in nature.
- As the child makes progress in the class less and less emphasis should be placed on readiness skills and more and more emphasis should be given on academic skills and the basic tool subjects such as reading, writing and arithmetic.
- Emphasis should be gradually placed on work-habits, vocational training, and family life education as the child makes progress from primary education to the secondary education. This should be particularly emphasized for older retarded students.

(v) Vocational training should actually pass through five phases, such as, vocational exploration, vocational evaluation, vocational training, vocational placement and follow up. In the phase of vocational exploration, the EMR student is familiarized with the nature of various occupations and their skill requirements. In the second phase the retarded student is exposed to experiences with different job skill in order to determine the vocational abilities and preferences of the student. In the third phase emphasis is given on developing job skills and on preparing the student for a range of occupations. This is the stage of on-the-job experiences. The fourth stage consists of locating a job for the student and placing him in the job. The last stage entails counseling and further training or replacement.

(vi) The EMR students should also be given knowledge about marriage, family life, child rearing, responsible parenthood, relationship and responsibilities of various members in the family etc. so that such students, when they grow up, will behave rationally and in a responsible way in relation to various aspects of marriage and family life. They should also be educated about civic rights and responsible citizenship.

8. ROLE OF THE TEACHER

A large number of mildly and some moderately retarded children do enter the regular primary schools. They remain unidentified and unnoticed for some years until their problems become so serious that they experience failure and frustration and later drop-out from the school. This calls for early identification, diagnosis and assessment and making instruction systematic and sensitive. The regular classroom teacher has to play a significant role in teaching such children in the regular classroom.

(i) The regular teacher should be familiar with the behavioural characteristics of MR children for purpose of identifying and referring them to the psychologist for assessment.

(ii) He should develop a positive and optimistic view about the educability of such children.

(iii) He should avoid as far as possible labeling the child, passing on damaging remarks and also see that the non-retarded peers behave in a positive way with the child.

(iv) He should create favourable conditions in his class and the school for social and academic integration of EMR children.

(v) He should constantly attempt to sequence learning tasks. Relatively complex units should be broken down into a hierarchy of sub-units and attempt should be made to teach one sub-unit at a time, help children to learn the sub-unit, and then to proceed to the next sub-unit.

(vi) The teacher should encourage retarded children to make use of verbal mediation in learning the tool subjects.

The retarded child should rehearse verbally what he is to learn and remember. Verbal mediation is a very useful learning strategy for learning concepts and problem-solving.

(vii) Retarded children do not know how to learn different subjects. Learning to learn is a useful technique for retarded children. The retarded child should be told verbally and exposed to models and tutoring by non-disabled peers for learning how to learn.

(viii) Many retarded children learn best by drill and repetition. Thus the teacher should give emphasis on drill and repetition in teaching language items and arithmetic skills.

(ix) Retarded children learn best through concrete experiences, play-way method, audio-visual aids and action-oriented teaching, etc. The regular teacher should, therefore, make use of concrete objects, story-telling, dramatization, music, dance, play situations, multisensory approach, coloured pictures, picture cards, word cards and toy materials in the teaching-learning situations.

(x) Many retarded individuals may be lacking in motivation. The regular teacher should look for ways to increase the motivation of such children. Interesting pictures and stories and novelty can increase motivation. However, progress should be from known to unknown and familiar to new experiences.

(xi) The retarded child should be given success experiences in learning tool subjects and social behaviours. Each experience of a retarded child should be followed by a consistent programme of reinforcement and feedback. Praise, recognition, reward, positive remarks, love and affection can have stimulating effects on the child in learning various skills.

(xii) The retarded child should be given opportunity to participate in classroom activities and cocurricular activities in the school. Such children can participate in drawing, painting, games and sports, music, songs and drama, gardening, beautification of school campus, celebrations and observation, etc.

(xiii) Continuous assessment should be made by the regular teacher about the child's level of functioning. This assessment may be either formal or informal.

(xiv) The regular teacher should seek the advice of the resource teacher whenever he has difficulty with the child's learning and behaviour. The resource teacher who is a consultant in the methodology of teaching the retarded children can help the regular teacher in teaching and behaviour modification techniques.

4

Learning Disability

1. MEANING OF LEARNING DISABILITY

Learning disability refers to an imperfect ability to listen, think, speak, read, write or do arithmetic. When learning problems are not primarily due to any impairment or environmental and economic disadvantages but due to a disorder in the psychological process or brain dysfunction we call it as learning disability.

Kirk (1962) says: "Learning disability refers to retardation, disorder, or delayed development in one or more of the processes of speech, language, reading, spelling, writing or arithmetic resulting from a possible cerebral dysfunction and/or emotional or behavioural disturbance and not from mental retardation, sensory deprivation, cultural or instructional factors."

The definition of learning disability adopted by National Advisory Committee on Handicapped Children (USA, 1968) is given as under:

"Children with specific learning disability exhibit a disorder in one or more of the basic psychological processes involved in understanding or using spoken or written language. These may be manifested in disorders of listening, thinking, talking, reading, writing, spelling or arithmetic. They include conditions which have been referred to as perceptual handicaps, dyslexia, development aphasia, etc. They do not include learning problems which are due primarily to visual, hearing, motor handicaps, mental retardation, emotional disturbances, or environmental disadvantages."

The National Joint Committee of Learning Disability (USA, 1981) gave the following definition of learning disability which is unanimously accepted at international level:

"Learning disability is a generic term that refers to a heterogeneous group of disorders manifested by significant difficulties in the acquisition and use of listening, speaking, reading, writing, reasoning or mathematical abilities. These disorders are intrinsic to the individual and presumed to be due to central nervous system dysfunction. Even though learning disability may occur concomitantly with other handicapping conditions (e.g., sensory impairment, mental retardation, social and emotional disturbance) or environmental influences (e.g., cultural differences, insufficient/inappropriate instruction, psychogenic factors) it is not the direct result of these conditions or influences."

From the definitions quoted above we can derive the meaning of learning disability as follows:

(i) Learning disability does not refer to any particular disorder. It is a general term that stands for a heterogeneous group of disorders.

(ii) It causes difficulties in listening, speaking, reading, writing or arithmetical computation.

(iii) It is not caused primarily due to visual handicap, hearing handicap, motor handicap, mental retardation, emotional disturbances or environmental disadvantages.

(iv) It is presumed to be caused due to cerebral dysfunction or minimal brain dysfunction.

(v) Learning disability causes a discrepancy between ability and achievement.

(vi) Learning disability is not the same condition as mental retardation. Mental retardation also causes learning problems. But the learning problems of mentally retarded children are due to low level of intelligence. By contrast learning disabled children possess average or above average intelligence. Their learning problems are due to cerebral dysfunction.

(vii) Learning disability is not the same as backwardness or slow learning. The backward child or the slow learner performs poorly in all academic subjects. Their problems may be due to low intelligence, disadvantaged social condition, emotional hazards or defective instruction. But the learning disabled child has difficulty in specific academic subjects such as speaking, reading, writing, etc. which may be due to brain dysfunction.

(viii) In terms of degree, learning disability may be of two types — mild LD and severe LD. The mild learning disabled can be educated in regular schools. Such children are to be found in regular schools. They are, however, difficult to identify at the initial stages. They face problems in learning basic academic skills. The severe learning disabled include those who manifest an inability to master basic academic skills (reading, writing etc.). Their problems may be due to brain dysfunction. It is difficult to integrate such children in regular schools.

2. TYPES OF LEARNING DISABILITY

Learning disability may occur in various forms such as reading disability, writing, disability communication disability comprehension disability and numerical disability, etc.

Reading Disability

Children suffering from reading disability are unable to read. There are two forms of this disability. In a mild form the affected person has difficulty in reading, but in severe cases of the impairment there is a total loss of the ability to read. This is sometimes also known as 'Word Blindness'. Children with the mild form of this disability are already in the general classroom. If identified early, proper help can be given and integration with their normal peers is also easier. The severely affected child will need intensive remedial exercises.

Writing Disability

The affected children are not able to write spontaneously. There are two forms of this impairment — the mild and severe. Children affected by the mild form have difficulty in learning to write legibly. They study in general schools. Their problems can be corrected if identified early and provided timely help. Those affected by the severe type of impairment can copy writing without distortion but they cannot write spontaneously. They are identified by their inability to learn to write. The severely affected children need remedial exercises and are thus hard to integrate in the academic areas.

Problems in Comprehending Communication

Children with this disability have a problem in communication through writing, speaking, or reading. Those affected by the mild form of this impairment have difficulty in understanding both the spoken and written words. The child finds it difficult to understand even signs and gestures. These children can be integrated if corrective measures are given in time. Otherwise, linguistic problems of articulation and fluency may develop. The severely affected child is unable to understand speech and written material, nor can he learn to speak, read and write. He is unable to communicate even through signs and gestures. Such children are difficult cases for integration. They need intensive remedial exercises.

Problems of Numerical Ability

The affected child has problems in calculations, even simple arithmetic, because of an inability to manipulate number relationships. Numerical inability is again of two kinds — mild and severe. Children with the mild form of this disability may already be studying in the general classroom. They are not easily identified at pre-primary levels. The disability becomes obvious when they start learning numbers and simple addition and subtraction. If identified early and with appropriate correction, they can study in the regular classes. If the problem is severe, the child will not be able to learn number symbols and their relationships. This is also termed as loss of arithmetic ability. The severe cases are difficult for integration and will require intensive remedial exercises.

3. CAUSES OF LEARNING DISABILITY

The causes of learning disability remain a mystery. Previously minimal brain dysfunction was considered to be the principal cause of learning disability. Even today cerebral dysfunction or central nervous system dysfunction is considered to be the cause of learning disability.

Different psychological processes are localized in different parts of the brain. If there is a disorder in any locality of the brain then the psychological function of that locality of the brain is disturbed and this causes disability with regard to speaking or reading or writing, etc.

Learning disability may occur concomitantly with visual impairment, hearing impairment, mental retardation, motor handicap or emotional disturbances. But impairment or retardation or emotional disturbance is not the primary cause of learning disability.

Contrary to the popular belief, learning disability is not caused due to instructional failure. Rather good instruction can reduce the problems caused due to learning disability.

4. SYMPTOMS OF LEARNING DISABILITY

Learning disabled children show the following symptoms which are mostly behavioural in nature:

(i) Difficulty in telling the time, order of days, etc.

(ii) Difficulty in recalling or repeating instruction correctly

(iii) Gets easily distracted by slight disturbances

(iv) Confuses between left and right

(v) Cannot sit still at a particular place even for a short period

(vi) Late submission of class work

(vii) Dull and slow in responding to others

(viii) Excessive inconsistency in the quality of performance

(ix) Difficulty in academic subjects (one or two subjects)

(x) Difficulty in reading, writing and arithmetic

(N.B.: Details of symptoms may be seen in the identification check list for LD children in Chapter 12).

5. PREVENTION AND CARE

There are mainly two approaches for the prevention and treatment of learning disability. These are: Medical-Neurological Approach and Psycho-Educational Approach.

Medical-Neurological Approach

The medical-neurological approach views the LD child as a patient afflicted with Minimal Brain Dysfunction (MBD). Such a child should be treated just like any other individual afflicted with a disease or injury. The most common symptom associated with MBD is hyperactivity. Thus quite logically, medication of some type would be sought to alleviate the child's symptoms. The most widely prescribed drugs to alleviate the symptom of hyperactivity are psycho-stimulants. Psycho-stimulants may bring about improvements in the behaviour of the LD child, but their effect on improving the learning of such children is not clearly established by research findings. Psycho-stimulant drugs can have a positive effect on a child's classroom behaviour, in reducing his activity level and making him more manageable and teachable but we cannot always count on them to remediate the child's learning problems. In addition to psycho-stimulant drugs, mega-vitamin therapy and diet management are sometimes recommended for LD children. But research findings on the effectiveness of mega-vitamin therapy and diet management are inconclusive. What is needed, therefore, is a behaviouristic approach or a psycho-educational approach which relies on the teacher's effectiveness in working with such children, motivating them and providing appropriate instruction to them.

Psycho-Educational Approach

The psycho-educational approach views the LD child not as a patient but as a learner waiting to be taught. From the psycho-educational perspectives, the LD children are to be identified early, assessed medically and psychologically to arrive at a correct diagnosis of their difficulties and weaknesses and provided with appropriate instruction and training in regular schools, resource rooms, special classes or special schools depending upon their degree of disability. There are various approaches for the education and training of LD children. All these approaches fall under five categories such as:

(i) Process training

(ii) Multi sensory approach

(iii) Environmental approach
(iv) Cognitive training
(v) Other special approaches and activities.

(i) *Process training*

Process training is based on the contention that learning academic subjects requires understanding the underlying psychological processes. Learning disabled children have a disorder in the psychological processes which underlie in understanding or using speech, in reading, writing, arithmetic, etc. Thus it may be of value to train the LD child in the psychological processes which underlie various academic subjects. For example, a LD child believed to have reading problems because of difficulties in visual perception will be trained in visual perception.

(ii) *Multi sensory approach*

Multi sensory approach is based on the assumption that the child will be more likely to learn if more than one of his senses is involved in the learning experiences. One such method is called the VAKT method (V stands for visual, A stands for auditory, K stands for kinesthetic and T stands for tactual). For example, the teacher asks the child to tell a story. The teacher writes down the words of the story on the blackboard. These words serve as material as the child learns to read. In learning the words, the child first sees the word (visual). He hears the teacher say the word (auditory). He says the word (auditory). Finally the child traces the word (kinesthetic and tactual).

(iii) *Environmental approach*

Learning disabled children are usually distractible and hyperactive. For such children an environmental approach is sometimes recommended by some educators. Environmental approach emphasizes reducing the irrelevant stimuli in the classroom environment which might distract the child's attention from the learning task. The classroom environment may be modified in the following ways as far as possible and as per necessity to make it free from unnecessary distraction:

- Sound-proofing of walls and ceilings.
- Carpeting.
- Opaque windows.
- Enclosed book cases and cupboards.
- Limited use of bulletin boards.
- Use of cubicles, three-sided work areas.
- Removing the pictures, calendar and other hanging objects from the walls.
- Ensuring a noise-free and in other ways a distraction-free environment outside the classroom.
- Enhancing the intensity of the teaching materials in terms of colour, size, and vividness.

(iv) *Cognitive training*

Many learning disabled children exhibit deficient problem-solving skills. They are likely to act impulsively rather than reflectively, responding quickly without considering the various alternatives. In order to reduce their impulsivity and to increase their reflectivity two techniques are found successful —

(i) Cognitive modeling and

(ii) Self-instructional training.

Cognitive modeling is sometimes known as meta cognition, meta memory and cognitive behaviour modification strategy. This approach is directed towards providing LD children with an awareness of how people learn or remember. In cognitive modeling the LD child is exposed to models (adults or peers) that tend to be more reflective so that he can imitate the model and learn the appropriate strategy. Through this technique the LD child is taught how to slow himself down before he reads a word or gives an answer, looks carefully, and then responds. In remembering, he is taught to group information into small bits or clusters, rehearses these by saying them over and over to himself and even uses mnemonic devices to aid in memory storages. Many LD children improve dramatically when they are simply made aware of the most effective way to learn and remember.

Modeling can also be combined with self-instructional training. In self-instructional training the impulsive child is encouraged to learn to develop verbal control of his behaviour. The following is an example:

- The teacher (adult model) performs a task (solving an arithmetic problem) while talking out to himself loudly,
- The child performs the same task under the direction of the teacher,
- The child whispers the instructions to himself as he goes through the task, and finally,
- The child performs the task while guiding his performance via private speech.

Through self-instructional training the LD child is helped to monitor his own performance in learning situation to be aware of his own approach to cognitive tasks.

(v) *Other special approach and techniques*

The LD children have characteristics which are unique to them. Although they are not visually impaired they have difficulty in visual perception. They have difficulty in visual reception, visual discrimination, and visual memory. Similarly although they are not auditory handicapped they have difficulty in auditory awareness, auditory discrimination, and auditory memory. They have problems in attention and retention. These difficulties hinder their acquisition of language, their ability to read and write, listening skills, etc. Hence, special training in these areas is very useful for LD children. The resource teacher can provide such training to the LD children in the resource room. The following approaches and activities are useful:

Listening Exercises

The LD children have problems of distractibility which hinder their acquisition of listening skills and hence their ability to follow directions. Listening exercises for such children are often helpful. One exercise involves having someone who is out of sight produce various sounds for the children to identify, such as bouncing a ball, clapping and shutting a door. Another exercise is, when the group goes for a walk, the children can be instructed to listen for common sounds, including a car running, a train chugging, or a bird singing. To improve comprehension of spoken words in children with listening problems, the teacher can give direction orally, beginning with short and simple ones and increasing the difficulty as the child progresses ('stand up, turn around, and then sit down'). Riddles can also be used to develop listening power and comprehension.

Discrimination Learning

The LD children have difficulties in discriminating one letter from another, one word from another and one number from another. Discrimination learning can be encouraged among such children for the above purpose. In discrimination learning children must be trained to attend to the similarities and differences between two letters, words, or numbers (e.g., b, d, p, q; 6, 9; 3, 8; hat, bat etc.) and then to make the correct response. In teaching such children letters, words, or numbers, these are to be written in the beginning in large sizes in crayon on news print paper. The children can trace the letters with their index fingers, while saying the letters, words, or numbers aloud. Visual and auditory attention is thus heightened in relation to these letters, words, or numbers. In order to improve their retention ability repetition or over learning may be encouraged.

Visual Reception Training

Visual reception can be encouraged by having children identify common objects by name and tell both their proper use and to whom each object belongs. They can be asked to stand in front of a mirror each day in the resource room and comment on what they see. Children can be given pictures to interpret in terms of objects seen, colours, size, motion, and other details.

Visual Memory Training

Visual memory can be developed by having children close their eyes and describe their clothing, a bulletin board in the room, or other children.

Spatial Training

Spatial training can be introduced by having children find the top, bottom, sides, and back of an object. The concepts of up, down, under, in, bigger, heavier, etc. can be demonstrated.

Auditory Awareness Training

Auditory awareness can be encouraged by having children remember various types of sounds heard during walk. The children can identify the source of each sound and give it an appropriate label. The teacher can hold a wrist watch to a child's ear at varying distances and train the child to listen and to raise a hand when the ticking is no longer audible. Directions can be whispered to the child at varying distances from each ear. Quiet periods can be held during which children are asked to listen to various sounds.

Auditory Discrimination Exercise

Auditory discrimination exercises can include hiding a ticking clock and asking a child to point to the direction of the clock. The teacher can tap several times on the desk and have the children listen, count to themselves and report the number of taps. While blind folded, a child can identify a classmate by his voice.

Auditory Memory and Sequencing Training

Auditory memory and sequencing can be developed by asking children to repeat directions, phone numbers, and clapping patterns. They can listen to nursery rhymes and songs and pick out details they will be asked to repeat afterwards. The teacher can tell simple jokes and have the children repeat them.

Remedial Instruction

The children with learning disability are benefited mostly from remedial instruction. Remedial instruction is nothing but good teaching with two definite and specific objectives, such as:

(i) Eliminating ineffective habits and re-teaching skills which have been incorrectly learned. This refers to remediation of defects.

(ii) Teaching for the first times those habits, skills and behaviours which have never been learned but should have been learned by the child to acquire academic skills. This refers to developmental teaching or development of increased competencies.

Remedial instruction requires proper diagnosis of a child's abilities and disabilities in specific school subjects, identifying skills and processes which require remediation, and then providing him just good teaching in areas of his weaknesses through systematic planning, individualized instruction, tutoring in one-to-one or small group situation, evaluating his progress periodically and, if necessary, re-teaching, encouraging intensive drill, practice or repetition and modifying the programme and adopting alternate materials and multi sensory approach. Most LD children improve their performance dramatically after exposure to remedial instruction in resource rooms which seems difficult in regular classroom settings. Remedial instruction in the resource room can vary from one hour every day to a half-day's programme regularly depending upon deficiencies and the amount of training required. It is to be emphasized that the sooner the remedial instruction starts in the elementary school the easier for the child to compensate his deficiencies, and the better for his later progress in upper classes.

6. ROLE OF THE TEACHER

Managing the LD Children

The child with learning disabilities needs individual tutoring in one or more of his areas of disability. Whether or not there is a resource teacher available will determine to a great extent how much of this instruction will be assumed by the regular class teacher. It is a fact that the regular classroom teacher and the resource teacher should have a cooperative working relationship. The regular teacher should work out with the resources teacher exactly what the duties of each of them are. "Who will be responsible for what" is a basic question that is sometimes never decided. However, the regular teacher has the following role to play:

(1) The regular classroom teacher who deals with children — abled and disabled — has much opportunity to observe their behavioural characteristics, identify the LD children and refer the suspected cases to the resource teacher for taking steps for assessment and diagnosis of their difficulties and deficiencies.

(2) Once he is sure of the specific deficiencies of such children he should plan his instruction in a systematic and sensitive way in consultation with the resource teacher. If there is no resource teacher in his school he must plan everything himself. He should remember that what LD children need is just good teaching. What is good teaching for LD children is also good teaching for normal children. There are many ways to describe good teaching for normal as well as LD children. The following principles may serve as guidelines for the regular teacher teaching normal and LD children in integrated settings (Hewett and Forness, 1984):

(i) *Expect the child to learn*: Teacher's expectation is reflected in the child's performance.

(ii) *Take nothing for granted*: Understand the child very patiently and carefully. The LD child may pretend to be attentive, motivated and seem to understand everything you are talking about, but in reality he does not.

(iii) *Bombard the senses*: Use multi-sensory approach to involve the child more completely in the teaching learning process.

(vi) *Load up the cues*: Have the child label and describe what is happening. Use a variety of distinctive elements and change them from time to time to bring novelty in experiences.

(v) *Make it vivid*: Increase the intensity of what is given to the child. Make it bigger, louder, more colourful, more imaginative, more exciting and more interesting. Be enthusiastic and animated.

(vi) *Report as often as necessary*: Assess the child's level of understanding. Be sure you have reached the child's level. Ask the child to tell you what have been presented. Repeat statements. Repeat directions. Don't be boring.

(vii) *Make it relevant*: Enter the child's world, Leave the examples given in the prescribed text books. Give them content that is familiar to them and part of their out-of-school life. Introduce local specific elements in your presentation.

(viii) *Make it concrete*: Use pictures, recordings and spoken words. These are fine. But don't stop there. Show real objects. Let the child touch, smell, manipulate and get direct impression and experience about concepts you are presenting.

(ix) *Surprise the child*: Present novel experiences. Use different materials and methods. Excite the child with stimulating experiences.

(x) *Emphasize the positive achievement*: Ignore the mistakes and at best make the child understand his mistakes, but in all cases recognize his positive achievement and tell it to others.

(xi) *Move sequentially*: Teach step by step.

(xii) *Review objectively*: Look back. Introspect what was your expectation. Modify your strategy and get ready to move ahead again as soon as possible.

(xiii) *Make it distraction-free*: Remove irrelevant stimuli from the classroom. Have distraction-free physical environment in and out of the classroom.

(xiv) *Be open to your colleagues*: Cooperate with them and seek their cooperation. Share and exchange experiences and learn from other's experiences.

Williams and Hounshell (1998) in their article *Enabling the Learning Disabled Teaching Strategies for Challenged*

Students say, "Many LD (learning disabled) students have the academic potential of non-disabled students but require some assistance in unveiling their potential and turning it into achievement".

Teaching Strategies:

- One of the most important things teachers should do is to provide support for risk taking and call attention to the successful work of a LD student without attaching the LD label.
- Making use of technology is advantageous, and it is a good idea to use computers as often as possible. Computers stimulate a variety of senses for LD students and are valuable.
- LD students are particularly receptive to television and video because they appeal to a number of senses.
- The music sounds and graphic often make learning come to life for LD students.
- LD students feel safe when they are watching a movie because there is no fear of being called on to answer a question or read aloud.

Classroom Organization

Teachers of LD students should also structure class time so that intense, laborious activities are interspersed with relaxing, enjoyable activities that allow students to move around. The teacher should take care of the following points:

- Desks arranged in clusters, however, are more conducive to promoting children's discussion or collaboration.
- When introducing new vocabulary words, repetition is important.
- To avoid confusing the child, teachers should plan assignments that focus on a primary task.
- It is better to start simply and add layers of complexity to LD students' assignments as the school year progresses.

Assessment Strategies

When assessing LD students, teachers should make assignments clear and grade using a qualitative scoring rubric. At the same time, when administering multiple choice tests, it is important that the answer choices are clear and that one choice stands out as the best answer.

Building Confidence

An excellent way to help LD students who are struggling with problems of low self-esteem is to entrust them with some duties and responsibilities. Taking care of a pet or a plant makes students feel important. They will see that their presence in the class is important not only in terms of potential academic contribution but also in maintaining the life of an organism. This attitude of the teacher will bring a dramatic shift in students' self-confidence.

5

Visual Impairment

1. MEANING OF VISUAL IMPAIRMENT

There are two prevailing ways of describing visual impairment: the legal definition and the educational definition. The legal definition is accepted by the medical profession whereas the educational definition is espoused by educators.

Legal/Medical Definition of Blindness

The legal definition involves assessment of visual acuity and field of vision. It is used to determine whether or not an individual qualifies for legal benefits. The American Medical Association (AMA) proposed this definition in 1934. This definition is now accepted by the American Foundation for the Blind (AFB) and other Blind Associations in different countries.

"A legally blind person is said to be one (i) who has visual acuity of 20/200 or less in the better eye even with correction, (ii) or whose field of vision is so restricted that it subtends an angle of 20° or less in the better eye after correction." Visual acuity is the ability of the eye to see distant objects clearly which is determined with the help of Snellen Chart. The visual acuity of 20/200 refers to the fact that what a blind person can see at 20 feet a person with normal vision sees at 200 feet (normal visual acuity is 20/200). A simple method of testing visual acuity is to see whether an individual can count fingers at one meter distance, if he cannot, he is blind. Similarly the normal field of vision is 180 degrees in front of the eye. The field of vision of blind person is restricted to 20 degrees or less in front of the eye. Normally a man looking straight ahead can see the finger when it leaves the straight line stretching to the left and right of the eyes. When the peripheral vision of an individual is lost and his field of vision is restricted he cannot see the finger when it leaves the front of the eye and stretches to the left or right side of the eye. He is also called legally blind.

There are some individuals who are known as partially blind or partially sighted. The partially sighted are those whose visual acuity falls between 20/70 and 20/200 in the better eye even after correction. At times, the term 'low vision' and 'partially sighted' are used as synonyms. But it is a wrong usage. Low vision is defined in terms of reduction in the clarity of vision, whereas partial sightedness is defined in terms of the distance through the Snellen Chart for educational purpose. This distinction is very important. Educational programmes can differ for such cases.

Educational/Functional Definition of Blindness

Many educators are disinterested in the legal or medical definition of blindness. Their argument is that visual acuity is not a very accurate predictor of how one will function or effectively use the remaining sight he has. A common misconception is that legally blind individuals have no sight. While a small percentage of the legally blind have absolutely no vision, the vast majority are able to see. Recognizing the limitations of the legal definition of blindness and partial sightedness, many have favoured an educational definition. For educational purpose, "the blind are those who are so severely impaired that they must be taught to read by Braille, while the partially sighted can read print by using magnifying glasses or books with large print".

The present trend is to classify visual handicap in terms of visual performance as follows:

(i) Normal or near-normal vision which means that the individual is able to perform all visual tasks adequately without special aids;

(ii) Low vision which means that the individual is unable to perform visual tasks that require detailed visions; and

(iii) Blindness which means that, without increased reliance on other senses, the individual is not able to perform tasks that normally require gross vision.

2. SYMPTOMS OF VISUAL IMPAIRMENT

Blindness is a visible disability. Hence by looking at the eyes of a person we can know that he is blind. But there are some blind persons whose eyes appear to be almost normal. The totally blind person has a variety of symbols — cane, thick or darkened glass, a guide, etc.

The low vision person or the partially-sighted person shows certain symptoms which may be behavioural or physical in nature. These symptoms of visual impairment are as follows:

(i) Crossed eyes

(ii) Red-rimmed, encrusted or swollen eye-lids

(iii) Watery eyes

(iv) Itching or burning of eyes

(v) Blurred or double vision

(vi) Dizziness, headaches, or nausea following close eye work

(vii) Rubbing eyes excessively

(viii) Covering one eye and tilting the head forward while reading

(ix) Holding objects or books close to the eye

(x) Blinking frequently

(xi) Squinting eye-lids together

(xii) Bumping into people or objects

(xiii) Excessive sensitivity to light

(xiv) Inability to participate in activities requiring distance vision.

3. CAUSES OF VISUAL IMPAIRMENT

Visual impairment may be hereditary or caused due to environmental hazards. In case of some blind children structural defects in the eyes are noticed from the moment of birth as a result of which these children cannot see. Structural defects may affect any part of the visual apparatus such as cornea, iris, retina, eye ball, optic nerve and choroids. If the pregnant mother suffers from diseases or takes drugs this may cause visual problems in the baby-to-be-born. Cataract, optic nerve atrophy, astigmatism, myopia, hyperopia, strabismus, glaucoma, retinitis pigmentosa, coloboma, retinoblastoma, retrolental fibroplasia, nystagmus, albinism, macular degeneration and hetrophoria are some of the diseases which cause visual impairment.

Visual impairment may also occur due to environmental factors such as accidents, and infectious diseases. Effect of poisonous substances and chemicals may also cause blindness. Deficiency of Vitamin A is a significant cause of visual problems. Lack of adequate illumination while reading causes strain in the eyes and visual problems in children.

4. PREVENTIVE MEASURES

Preventive measures aim at preventing visual problems from becoming a serious one. If a child is born blind we can do very little to prevent his problems from becoming a serious one. But if visual problems are due to environmental factors the following measures can be taken:

(i) Children must be protected from facing accidents. They should be particularly trained in road safety measures.

(ii) If children suffer from infectious diseases they should be treated immediately by doctors, and not by indigenous methods. Neglect in the treatment of infectious diseases like chicken pox and small pox may cause loss of vision.

(iii) Children should be protected from poisonous substances. Safety measures in the home and the school laboratory can prevent children from reaching poisonous substances. Children should be guarded and guided properly while using crackers on festive occasions.

(iv) Children should be provided adequate amount of Vitamin A in their diet. Vitamin A is available in milk, eggs, butter, pure ghee, fish, green vegetables like carrots, cabbage, cauliflower, beats, etc.

(v) Arrangement for adequate illumination should be made in the classroom for low vision children so that these children can be prevented from facing further problems.

(vi) Children should be subjected to regular medical check up for eye diseases and watery, itching eyes during winter seasons.

(vii) Children's eyes should be protected from dusts and other external substance as these substances may cause damage to the eyes.

5. EDUCATION AND TRAINING OF VISUALLY IMPAIRED

Every child whether normal, hearing impaired or visually impaired has a right to appropriate education and training. Every society must grant this right to the visually impaired so that they become useful members of the society.

The visually impaired children constitute a heterogeneous group. Some are totally blind, some are partially sighted, some low vision and some one-eyed. The care and training of such children must therefore match with the nature of their loss of vision. Care, training and education of such children must be the joint responsibility of parents, teachers and community members.

Most experts agree that, for the most part, the visually impaired should be educated in the same general way as the sighted following the same general principles. But some modifications in the teaching methodology may be needed.

(i) **Use of remaining sight.** The visually impaired children will have to rely on sensory modalities other than vision to acquire information. But they are to be encouraged to use their remaining sight or residual vision as much as possible. This is particularly advisable for partially sighted children.

(ii) **Closed circuit television.** A closed circuit television reader has been developed to aid partially sighted students in Western countries. A camera with a zoom lens photographs parts of a page of print and projects a magnified image on the television screen. The student moves the book while reading so that the appropriate portion of the page is magnified. The size of the magnified print can be controlled.

(iii) **Magnifying glasses and Hand magnifiers.** The partially sighted and low vision children should be encouraged to read the print through magnifying glasses or hand magnifiers which present enlarged images of print.

(iv) **Large print materials.** The partially sighted and low vision children should be provided with large print materials. Large print books are simply volumes that contain print that is considerably larger than usual. The most common type recommended for such children is 18 point type or letters approximately one-eighth inch high. Such print reduces reading speed. However large print may be useful in case of reference books, dictionaries, mathematics and maps.

(v) **Braille.** Visually impaired children who cannot read regular print even with magnifying or large print materials should be trained to use Braille. Braille is a basic system of reading and writing for the blind. It consists of a six-dot cell that provides for sixty three different characters. 26 combinations of dots are used for 26 letters of the alphabet. The remaining 37 combinations represent punctuation signs and contractions that allow for shortening or abbreviating words. In some ways Braille is a system of shorthand since each word is not spelled out letter for letter. As a result blind children have difficulty with spelling because of the frequent abbreviations used in the Braille system. In addition to Braille code for reading and writing there are codes for music, mathematics, computer science and chemistry.

Braille has many disadvantages. Books and periodicals printed in Braille are very bulky, expensive and take up a great deal of storage space. Moreover, Braille materials are not always available for all subjects and in all languages.

(vi) **Talking calculator.** Both the partially sighted and the blind may profit from a talking calculator. In the talking calculator, numerical entries are read aloud to the student through an earplug. Blind children may profit more from the talking calculator in learning Mathematics.

(vii) **Tape recordings.** Reading materials from both standard texts and books for leisure reading can be transcribed by the teacher and presented to the blind that usually profit from audio-aural cues more than visual cues. The use of tape recording is gaining in popularity as a method of teaching language, history, geography, science etc. The blind can cover the same material much more quickly.

The whole gamut of the curriculum for children in school is centered on two significant aspects — the opportunity and the experience. Often children are provided with opportunities, but the mere provision of opportunities does not mean the acquisition of experience.

Sighted children have an edge over blind children in the acquisition of knowledge through experience. Sighted children acquire rich experience in a natural way. They learn the experience as a 'whole'. But the learning of blind children is in 'pieces' of information. There is thus a need for different approaches to the curriculum for blind children.

(viii) **General curriculum with modified experience.** Many experts agree that blind children should be educated in the same general way, following the same general principles and along with sighted children in the regular schools or in integrated settings. The curriculum for blind children should be more like that of the sighted children. Most information is received by the visually handicapped child through touch and hearing. Hence, these experiences must be planned to facilitate the acquisition of near normal experience acquired by sighted children through vision. Multi sensory experiences are to be provided to blind children to acquire near-normal experiences.

The visual experience should be converted into non-visual experience for concept development of blind children. For this purpose the teacher should follow the following steps:

- Give duplicate experience as far as practicable.
- Modify the experience in terms of concept, method of display, type of materials used and response expectations from the child.
- Substitute the lesson to a different lesson which as

closely as possible approximates that presented to the sighted children.

- Omit a lesson sometimes if the former three steps are not possible.

(ix) **The plus curriculum.** The plus curriculum is always recommended for blind children. The plus curriculum is not something extra as the name may appear to indicate. It is compensatory. It contains skills and competencies which, if developed early, result in the learning of the general curriculum meant for sighted children. The special areas of the plus curriculum are as follows:

- Braille
- Orientation and Mobility
- Daily living skills
- Sensory training
- Social skills
- Use of equipment like braillers and abacus.

(x) **Co-curricular activities.** Visually impaired children should be given the opportunity for participation in co-curricular activities in the school. Keeping in view their visual impairment and their possibilities in performing co-curricular activities the following activities are recommended for them:

Singing, playing instruments, debating, composing poems (The visually impaired children may take part in all these activities with sighted children).

Games and sports with provision of auditory cues for visually impaired child (for examples, a bell ball can replace the ordinary ball used by sighted children in football match).

Since visually impaired children demonstrate slow pace of performance in co-curricular activities, in no case should they be compared with sighted children. The approach in this case should be purely on an individual basis.

6. ROLE OF THE TEACHER

Managing the Visually Impaired

Visually impaired children are now attending regular classes in increasing number. Excepting few modifications they are pursuing the same general curriculum in regular schools. The resource teacher is there to provide resource room instruction to the visually impaired children. But as we all know education of handicapped children is the joint responsibility of the resource teacher and the regular teachers. In fact education of handicapped children is ultimately the responsibility of regular teachers. The resource teacher is a support teacher. Regular teachers should therefore know how to handle such children.

(i) The visually impaired child has the same right to education as the sighted children. But very often blind children are denied the opportunity to receive education in general schools. In fact, if a blind child has completed his preparation in a special school there is no point why he should not be enrolled in a general school.

(ii) While planning to provide education to visually impaired children in the regular classroom the regular teacher should contact and consult with the resource teacher. The resource teacher who is a specialist in the methodology of special education can guide the regular teacher in the teaching-learning process,

(iii) The regular teacher should ask the visually impaired child to care for his own material as part of his effort to foster a sense of independence.

(iv) He may ask a sighted child in the class to act at times as a guide as long as the visually disabled pupil does not become too dependent upon him.

(v) The blind child should be treated in the same way as his sighted peers. The same experience should be provided to both the sighted and the visually impaired children.

(vi) The regular teacher should encourage healthy interaction between the visually impaired and the sighted children.

(vii) Visually impaired children should be encouraged by the regular teacher to participate in as many activities of the school as possible. If it is not possible for the visually impaired child to join with the rest of the class in some activities the regular teacher should plan alternate activities for him.

(viii) The regular teacher should give the same kinds of special tasks to the visually impaired that are given to other children.

(ix) The regular teacher should ensure a proper physical environment in the classroom for the partially sighted children. Adequate illumination is a must. The seating arrangement is also very important. The child should be seated so that he can best see the chalkboard and other materials. Glossy pictures should be avoided. Visual materials should be free from distracting background materials. The teacher should write on the chalkboard in large and clear letters. In addition, because of the great amount of visual attention the child must maintain frequent rest periods as may be necessary.

(x) While teaching, most teachers use many non-verbal signs/cues which are inappropriate for the visually impaired. It is therefore important for the teacher to verbalize his intents to the visually impaired child.

(xi) Initially the direction, location and the distance of various objects, rooms and other essential things should be made clear to the visually impaired child.

(xii) The important thing in teaching visually impaired children is to help them learn the maximum possible while at the same time encouraging their sense of independence and accomplishment. The purpose of assimilating them into the regular classroom is to help them learn to function as effectively as possible in the world and the teacher's role in this regard is a vital and challenging one.

6

Hearing Impairment

1. WHAT IS HEARING IMPAIRMENT?

Hearing impairment refers to a defect in or damage to the hearing mechanism. This defect or damage may occur in any part of the ear — outer ear or middle ear or inner ear. Hearing impairment leads to hearing disability or loss of hearing. Hearing disability or loss of hearing may range in severity from mild to moderate to profound. A person may become deaf or hard-of-hearing depending upon the nature of impairment and the degree of hearing loss. According to USA Public Law (94-142), "Deaf means a hearing impairment which is so severe that the child is impaired in processing linguistic information through hearing, with or without amplification, which adversely affects his educational performance. Hard-of-hearing means a hearing impairment, whether permanent or fluctuating, which adversely affects a child's educational performance but which is not included under the definition of deaf".

A child may be born with some impairment in the hearing mechanism or the impairment may occur after birth due to infection, disease and obstruction or damage due to accident. Due to hearing impairment the child becomes unable to hear, speak and acquire language. Thus, a child may become dumb largely because he is deaf.

2. TYPES OF HEARING IMPAIRED

The hearing impaired children have been classified under various sub-groups from various angles.

(a) **Types based on the degree of hearing loss.** Depending on the degree of hearing loss the hearing impaired children are classified into two groups such as the deaf, and the hard-of-hearing.

The total inability to hear is called deafness. The deaf are those who, even with the best auditory training, cannot learn to understand speech mainly through hearing. The hard-of-hearing children have some residual degree of hearing and can be benefited through amplification. They are those children in whom the sense of hearing, although defective, is functional with or without a hearing aid.

The hearing impaired children are also classified into the following five sub-groups depending on the degree of hearing loss or hearing sensitivity. Hearing loss or hearing sensitivity is measured in decibels (dB).

Hearing impairment categories based on the degree of hearing loss as per the Ministry of Welfare (Govt. of India), Notification No. 4283HW, dt. 6.8.86 are given in table 6.1:

TABLE 6.1

Degree of Hearing Loss in Terms of dB Level and Percentage

Category	Type of Impairment	dB Level in Better ear	Percentage of impairment
I	Mild	dB 26 to 40	Less than 40%
II	Moderate	dB 41 to 55	40% - 50%
III	Severe	dB 56 to 70	50% - 75%
IV	Profound	dB 71 to 90	75% - 100%
	Near total Deafness	dB 91 and above	100%
	Total deafness	No hearing	100%

Decibels (dB) mean a unit of relative loudness of a sound. Zero decibels (0 dB) designate the point at which people with normal hearing can detect even the faintest sound. Each succeeding number of dB indicates a certain degree of hearing loss. Decibels are found from audiograms. An audiogram is a graphic representation of the weakest sound that the individual being tested can hear at each of several different levels of pitch (Hz).

(b) **Types based on age of onset.** Hearing impairment may occur since birth or it may be acquired at any age in life. Thus, depending on the age of onset we have two groups of hearing impaired children such as:

Congenitally deaf

Adventitiously deaf

The congenitally deaf child is one who is born with impaired hearing. Such a child has not heard any sound or speech. The adventitiously deaf child is one who is born with normal hearing. He has acquired speech, but later lost hearing ability due to infection, disease or some damage to the hearing mechanism.

(c) **Types based on language experience.** Hearing impaired children are also classified into the following two groups depending upon the language experience they have acquired:

Pre-lingual deaf

Post-lingual deaf

The pre-lingual deaf child is one who is born with little or no hearing. He has suffered the loss of hearing early in infancy before speech and language patterns are acquired. Post-lingual deaf children are those who had language exposure for some time but later they became deaf owing to environmental factors. The speech of pre-lingual deaf child is slow and laboured and is usually accompanied by a high pitch. Prolonged vowels, rhythmic abnormality, excessive nasality, imperfect joining of consonants and defective articulation are some of the characteristics of their speech.

(d) **Types based on the location of the problem.** Hearing loss is also classified into three types depending upon the location of the hearing problem or defect. These are—

Conductive loss,

Sensori-neural loss and

Mixed loss.

If the hearing problems are located in the outer ear and the middle ear it is called conductive loss. If the problems arise out of the defects in the inner ear it is called sensory-neural loss. A combination of conductive loss and sensory-neural loss is called mixed loss.

(e) **Central deafness.** In addition to the above types of hearing loss there is another type of hearing loss called the central deafness. When the sound vibrations reach the inner ear, the inner ear transforms these vibrations and sends them to the auditory centre in the brain. The brain perceives these sounds meaningfully and understands the message. If there is any defect in the auditory centre in the brain we cannot hear anything. This type of hearing loss is known as central deafness.

Among all these classifications the one based on the degree of hearing loss — Mild, Moderate, Severe and Profound — is widely accepted for integrated education purpose. Children with mild to moderate loss of hearing can be integrated in regular schools.

3. SYMPTOMS OF HEARING IMPAIRMENT

Hearing impaired children are not easily noticeable unless someone talks to them. However these children show certain symptoms which are as follows:

(i) Observable deformity of the ear,

(ii) Discharge from the ear,

(iii) Frequent pain in the ear,

(iv) Scratching the ear frequently,

(v) Asking for repetition of instruction,

(vi) Turning the head frequently towards the speaker,

(vii) Inability to follow instruction,

(viii) Focusing on the speaker's face while listening to him.

(ix) Restlessness and inattention,

(x) Asking for help from peers for taking notes in the classroom.

If a child shows any four or five symptoms, hearing impairment can be suspected.

4. CAUSES OF HEARING IMPAIRMENT

Hearing impairment may be caused both by heredity and environmental factors:

(i) In some cases hearing impairment is inherited from parents. Particularly the congenitally deaf children who are born with impaired hearing inherit the impairment from the parents. Similarly the pre-lingual deaf children are born with little or no hearing. Pre-lingual deafness is also inherited from parents.

(ii) Structural defects in the hearing mechanism also cause hearing impairment. Structural defects may occur in any part of the hearing mechanism — outer ear, middle ear, inner ear or the auditory centre in the brain. Conductive loss which is the result of defects in the outer ear and middle ear, sensory-neural loss which is the result of defect in the auditory centre of the brain are largely hereditary in nature.

(iii) Hearing impairment may be also caused due to environmental factors such as infection and disease in the ear, injury or damage to the hearing mechanism due to accident, sudden blow to the ear and high amplification of sound close to the ear.

5. PREVENTIVE MEASURES

As discussed earlier hearing impairment can occur due to hereditary factors or due to environmental factors. In other words, hearing loss can be noticed from birth or it may be acquired after birth. The following preventive measures are useful to prevent hearing problems from becoming a serious one and to prevent hearing impairment among young children:

(i) Hearing impaired children should be encouraged to use hearing aid regularly. A single cord hearing aid should be used by the child if one ear is affected. If both the ears are affected then a V cord hearing aid should be prescribed for him.

(ii) While using hearing aid care must be taken to see that the battery is in working condition and that the amplification is appropriate for the amount of loss of hearing.

(iii) Diseases and infections in the ear should be immediately treated by specialist doctors. Indigenous methods of treating ear diseases such as pouring oil in the affected ears should be avoided.

(iv) Discharges, dusts and other substance in the ear should be cleared regularly with the help of sterilized ear sticks. Match sticks, unused refills and dirty sticks should not be put in the ear as they may cause injury to the ear or infection in the ear.

(v) While bathing in ponds the ears must be covered with palms so as to prevent dirts from entering into the ears which may cause infection.

(vi) Parents and teachers should not give a blow to the tender ears of young children or give a strong slap to the ears of young children as this may cause damage to the hearing mechanism.

6. EDUCATION AND TRAINING OF HEARING IMPAIRED

Hearing-impaired children differ from one another in many ways. They may differ in the degree and type of hearing loss, the age of onset of deafness, intelligence, parents', ability and attitude, home environment and the nature and amount of their home-training, if any. The care, training and education of such children, therefore, must depend on these factors mentioned above.

Every child, whether he is abled or disabled, has a right to education and every society must grant this right to the hearing-impaired children to receive appropriate training and education so that they become useful members of the society and participate in nation building instead of being a burden for the parents. The care and training of hearing-impaired children should match with their degree and type of loss. Moreover, care and training of hearing-impaired children should be the joint responsibility of the home, school, community, health and social welfare personnel.

Parents' responsibility: Care and training of a hearing impaired child should start in the home. Parents, siblings and other members of the family have a major and crucial role to play in the care and training of the disabled child. Since parents' responsibility in the care and training of hearing impaired children is beyond the scope of our discussion this will not be discussed in detail in this section. However, few hints are necessary here. Parents' responsibility lies in:

(i) Early identification of hearing impairment based on the child's developmental responses to sound and speech,

(ii) Referring the suspected cases to the ENT specialists and the audiologist for assessment,

(iii) Accepting the impaired child and showing love and affection to him like other normal children in the family,

(iv) Consulting the specialists and the teachers and sharing the responsibility for the training of the child,

(v) Encouraging the child to use the hearing aid regularly,

(vi) Teaching the child verbal skills, writing skills, reading skills and stimulating their language development,

(vii) Encouraging self-playing, playing with siblings, playing with the peer groups and developing singing, saying rhymes, listening to stories and the habit of sharing and taking turns,

(viii) Creating conditions for social normalization of the child in the home,

(ix) Acting as per the advice of specialists,

(x) Preparing the child for integration in the school.

School's responsibility: In addition to parents' responsibility the school has a major responsibility in the care and training of hearing-impaired children. The major problem of hearing-impaired children lies in their deficiency in speech and language development and communication. There are three methods of training deaf children — the oral method, the manual method and the total communication approach. Finger spelling and sign language are examples of manual method. Lip reading or speech reading and auditory training are examples of oral method. The manual method is appropriate for severely and profoundly deaf children. The oral method is best suited for mild-to-moderately hearing handicapped children. Since hearing-impaired children who are enrolled in general schools are mostly mildly or moderately handicapped we will discuss lip reading and auditory training in detail. In addition to these, techniques of curriculum adaptation and teaching strategies should also be kept in mind.

(a) **Sign Language.** The main problem faced by hearing impaired persons is effective communication. The speech of a profoundly deaf person is hardly intelligible to hearing persons. For this purpose sign language is extensively used by most of them. Sign language is a system of gestures that is used to convey general ideas or thoughts. There are a variety of sign languages. Today a standard set of signs known as American Sign Language (Ameslan) is used by many deaf people. Profoundly deaf children who have virtually an inability to communicate through verbal language and whose speech is not intelligible should be trained to use non-verbal sign and gestures or more particularly the Ameslan. This is possible only by specially trained teachers in special schools.

(b) **Finger Spelling.** Profoundly deaf children who have had some schooling and education can be taught finger spelling to achieve some facility in communication amongst themselves and also with the hearing-speaking world. This is inevitable since the speech of a profoundly deaf person is hardly intelligible to hearing person despite the fact that he may have acquired some language and is capable of using words or sentences.

Although educated deaf persons could communicate by resorting to writing, it is not practical to move around with paper and pencil all the time. Hence, the need arises for finger spelling. Finger spelling is nothing but writing in the air with configurations of fingers. The words for which there are no signs (such as names of persons) are often finger spelled. Thus, finger spelling can be described as a manual representation of written language. Put simply, finger spelling is the use of finger positions to represent the letters of the alphabet. Alphabet is a system of letters. To some extent finger spelling resembles the printed letter of the alphabet.

In India mainly two types of finger spelling are used. Both are based on English alphabet. Each letter (A to Z) has a distinct shape. The English finger spelling is performed either with one hand as the American system, or with both hands as in the British system. The Indian Manual Alphabet named as "Kara Pallavi" has also been developed for use in Indian context. It is based on the American one-hand alphabet system.

When finger spelling, the palm of the hand should face the audience. The hand should not block a view of the lips as it is important to see lip movements as well. Ideally the words should be spelt at shoulder level. Finger spelling can be taught in special schools for the deaf.

(c) **Speech Reading (Lip Reading).** Speech reading is sometimes referred to as lip reading. Lip reading refers to observing the lip movements or movement of the mouth of the speaker and understanding what is being told by the speaker. But in speech reading the deaf child not only observes the lip movements of the speaker but also uses the visual stimuli in the environment to comprehend spoken messages. Thus, speech reading is more comprehensive and a more accurate term than lip reading. The major goals of speech reading are:

(i) Observing the lip movements and facial expression of the speaker;

(ii) Observing the visual stimuli in the environment;

(iii) Understanding what is being spoken.

Principles of Speech Reading

(i) Teach the child to pay attention to and obtain meaning from the environment.

(ii) Teach the child to expect certain kinds of messages in certain kinds of situations.

(iii) Teach the child to associate specific movements of the mouth with specific sounds.

(iv) Relate your facial expressions directly to the content and tone of the words you are using.

(v) Engender in the child an awareness of his visual surrounding by showing the child pictures/objects and then asking questions about them.

(vi) Speak to the deaf or the hard-of-hearing child as often as possible.

(vii) Speak slowly.

(viii) Speak clearly.

(ix) Speak in a natural way without exaggeration.

(x) See that your face is clearly visible to the child.

(xi) See that your face is illuminated while you are speaking to the child.

(xii) Stand or sit in front of the child while you are speaking to him.

(xiii) Look at his face while you are speaking to him.

(xiv) Don't smoke or chew betels while speaking to the child.

(xv) Ensure that the matter you are talking about is known to the child.

(xvi) Don't speak loudly close to the hearing aid.

(d) **Auditory Training.** The growing body of evidence supports the belief that almost no child is born with absolutely no hearing sensation. A hearing impaired child has some residual hearing ability. Auditory training is the procedure of teaching the deaf or hard-of-hearing child to make use of his residual hearing ability. It has three major goals:

(i) Development of awareness of a variety of sounds, including speech in his environment;

(ii) Development of the ability to make gross discriminations among non-verbal or environmental sounds;

(iii) Development of the ability to discriminate among speech sounds under high and low redundancy conditions (High redundancy refers to speech consisting of simple, familiar subject matter with little distraction from the environment. Low redundancy approximates more closely the way in which speech is used in the natural environment).

Principles of Auditory Training

(i) Formal auditory training is essential to teach the deaf child to make use of his remaining hearing ability.

(ii) The less severe the hearing loss, the more auditory training should be emphasized.

(iii) It is important to begin auditory training early.

(iv) Auditory training should better be provided with a hearing aid.

(v) Auditory training, even without a hearing aid, should be begun as soon as it is determined that a child is deaf.

(vi) Auditory training appears to be more effective through mutual reinforcement, when hearing is combined with vision and/or touch.

(vii) Auditory training should be geared to a child's auditory capabilities. This requires frequent assessment of his hearing capacity.

(viii) Auditory training should be based on experiences that are meaningful.

(e) **The Total Communication Method.** A recent development in the methodology of teaching communication skills to deaf children is the total communication method. This method combines all the means and methods — speech reading, finger spelling, sign language, auditory training, etc. The idea is to teach communication to the hearing impaired child by any means. The oral method or the manual method is not suitable to meet the needs of all hearing impaired children. Hence, instead of debating which method is more appropriate to a particular hearing impaired child a combination of different methods can be adopted which will meet the needs of all hearing impaired children. This method is becoming very popular in various schools.

(f) **Curriculum Adaptation and Teaching Strategies.** The centrally sponsored scheme of IED visualizes that the same learning experiences will be provided to both the disabled and the normal children studying in the IED schools. But hearing-impaired children, like other disabled children, have difficulty in understanding some of the content areas which include more verbal concepts. It is, therefore, necessary to adapt the curriculum to the needs and difficulties of such children. The following principles are important:

(i) While adapting the curriculum to the needs of hearing impaired children, the objectives of instruction should remain same for hearing-impaired and normal children. Only learning materials and methodology may be modified. The learning material and methodology have to be modified in such a way that it will not disturb the majority of normal children studying in the class.

(ii) Ideally speaking the ratio between hearing impaired and normal children in a particular classroom should be 1:5 in Indian context. The hearing-impaired children should be asked to sit in the front benches/in the front line along with normal children. This will help them to hear better. If a hearing-impaired child has to sit on any side (left or right side) in the front line then the teacher must arrange to ensure that the better ear of the child is towards the class and the teacher.

(iii) In an integrated setting the normal peers are to be encouraged to participate in the education and training of hearing-impaired. They can participate in correction of specific learning problems, teaching spelling, articulation, new concepts and curricular activities.

(iv) The teacher has to see that the hearing-impaired child is using the hearing aid regularly in the class. He has also to check, from time to time, the working condition of the hearing aid.

(v) The hearing-impaired children need to develop adequate speech and language patterns. Supportive aids like recorded tapes, articulation charts, speech trainer, photo album, concrete objects and other visual cues should be used for speech training, speech correction and language learning.

Adjustment of material and methodology can also be done with resource room teaching. The teacher should identify the learning difficulty of the hearing-impaired subject-wise and suggest remedial exercises accordingly. These exercises should be organized by the resource teacher outside the class by a special arrangement of the time table within the normal school hour. For example, the hearing-impaired child may have difficulty in learning to speak certain sounds such as 'bh', 'th', 'dh', etc, and discriminate certain sounds. For developing sound discrimination and teaching the child to speak certain sounds the resource teacher should give corrective exercises to the hearing-impaired child in the resource room. Adequate training in speech correction with the help of speech trainer, recorded tapes, photo album and articulation chart in the resource room will be very useful.

Hearing-impaired children have faulty patterns of language learning and usage. They generally have disarticulation problems and as a result they also spell words wrongly. They generally write in the way they speak. For example, they may say and write 'tigre' for 'tiger' and 'klass' for 'glass'. For correcting such problems, the teacher should give more visual cues on articulation of the sounds used for each word. This will help them to learn to speak and spell words correctly. The teacher may provide additional work book for writing. In addition to the above, the teacher should give emphasis on story telling, short question and answer method in the teaching and learning of language and speech.

(vi) The hearing-impaired children have difficulty in learning abstract concepts and difficult words. The holistic method based on fingers, pictures, and concrete experiences, audio-visual aids, role playing and dramatization should be used for teaching new, difficult and abstract concepts. Action-oriented situations should be given for teaching emotional concepts like happiness, unhappiness, crying, shouting etc.

(vii) Hearing-impaired children have the primary difficulty of learning language and speech. Since language learning is basic to learning all other subjects the hearing-impaired children, owing to their difficulty in learning language, have problems in learning other subjects. If the hearing-impaired children can be helped to learn the language and speech patterns their problems in learning other subjects can be sorted out easily by the teacher.

(viii) The resource teacher should keep a record of what the child knows, what he can do and what he cannot do, plan his lessons according to the educational needs of the child, guide other teachers in teaching the various lessons, assess periodically the progress made by the child, encourage, motivate and provide feedback to the child regularly.

7. ROLE OF TEACHER

Managing hearing-impaired children: The regular teacher may at one time or another have hard-of-hearing children in his class. He has an important role to play in managing such children in the class:

(i) There are behavioural characteristics or symptoms of hearing impairment which the regular classroom teacher should watch for. He should refer suspected cases or advise parents to consult with specialist doctors for medical treatment.

(ii) The very presence of one or two hearing-impaired children in the class of 35 to 40 hearing students is likely to create a feeling of uneasiness in the minds of the class teacher. If he has no previous knowledge of such children and their handicap he will ask himself, "How will I teach them?" Certainly they create problems for him. He should, therefore, attend short-term training or orientation course so that he will know the implications of their handicap, understand their educational needs, and make necessary adjustments so that such children feel at home and secure in the class.

(iii) He should develop a positive attitude and show love and affection towards such children. The impact of the teacher's behaviour will be reflected in the behaviour of his peers.

(iv) He should arrange seats for them in the front row of the room, preferably on one side, so that they obtain a better view of both the teacher and the classmates.

(v) He should keep the auditory and visual distracters to a minimum. Although such distraction may not always be under the control of the teacher, excessive noise from the hall, other rooms, and outside should be eliminated, especially when he is talking. It should be remembered that environmental noises are also a problem for the child with a hearing aid, since all noises are amplified for him.

(vi) To optimize the child's opportunities to speech-read, the teacher should try to maintain a distance of about six feet between himself and the child. Standing too close can be a hindrance because it prevents the child from being able to observe situational cues.

(vii) The teacher should see that the hearing-impaired child uses the hearing aid regularly and that the hearing aid is in perfect condition. If he notices any disorder or wrong use steps should be taken to rectify the defect and ensure correct use.

(viii) The teacher should speak naturally and follow other principles of speech-reading and auditory training.

(ix) The teacher should attempt to standstill when talking, because excessive movement adds to the difficulty of speech-reading.

(x) The teacher should be careful not to turn his back to the class and talk while writing on the black-board.

(xi) New vocabulary should be introduced both orally and in writing.

(xii) The teacher should encourage the child to ask questions when he is unsure of what is being told. When it is necessary to repeat something the teacher should try to rephrase the instruction. There are some words and phrases that are easier to lip read than others, and rephrasing increases the chances that the child will be exposed to words he can comprehend.

(xiii) The teacher should make every effort to use visual aids in the instructional process. The use of transparencies on an overhead projector (if possible) is a good way to do this. Simply writing instructions or new vocabulary items or important points on the black-board is another good method.

(xiv) The teacher should follow the teaching strategies and adapt the curriculum to the needs of the hearing-impaired child.

(xv) He should give opportunity to the hearing-impaired child to participate in various co-curricular activities in the class and the school depending on his abilities and interest.

(xvi) If the regular teacher has difficulty in managing or teaching the child in the class he should consult with the resource teacher and act accordingly.

7

Speech Handicap

1. MEANING OF SPEECH HANDICAP

Speech handicap refers to the abnormal speech patterns or disorders in speech which cannot be understood by the listeners. In other words when speech becomes unintelligible and irregular it is called speech handicap. But all unintelligible speech is not speech handicap. For example, if an individual speaks in Hindi to non-Hindi speaking people his speech becomes unintelligible to these non-Hindi speaking people. But this is not speech handicap. Only when speech is not understood by native speakers of that particular language we may call it speech handicap. Similarly under the state of intense emotional disturbance an individual's speech may be disturbed and irregular. But if under normal conditions his speech is well understood by the listeners then we cannot call it speech handicap.

Speech handicap creates difficulties for the speaker to communicate his feelings and ideas to others. This is why speech handicap is often called as communication handicap or communication disorder. A child with speech handicap is like any other normal child, he can do and perform tasks like other non-handicapped child, but he has difficulties in situations which involve speech and verbal ability.

Speech handicap is largely linked with hearing handicap. That is why deaf children become dumb. When a child becomes deaf by birth he does not get opportunity to hearing others and learning the speech patterns. He develops speech handicap.

2. TYPES OF SPEECH HANDICAP

Speech handicap does not refer to any specific handicap. The term speech handicap is a complex one which stands for different types of disorders related to speech and language. The following are the different types of speech handicap:

(i) Articulatory disorders which involve substitution, omissions, distortions and addition of sounds. There is a difficulty in pronunciation of words distinctly or clearly.

(ii) Defects of voice which involve problems in vocal quality (breathiness, hoarseness, or huskiness), vocal pitch (high pitch), and vocal intensity.

(iii) Stuttering and stammering. In stuttering there is frequent and severe disorder of rhythm or fluency, hesitating in speech, repetition of letters and words and lingering on them. Stammering involves faltering or stumbling in speech.

(iv) Cleft palate speech which involves structural defects in the lips, particularly the upper lip.

(v) Delayed speech. There are normal milestones of speech and language development. If speech and language development is delayed it creates problems in communication of ideas and feelings.

(vi) Speech defects associated with hearing-impairment such as dumbness.

It is worthwhile to state the views of B.F. Skinner regarding speech and language development of children at different ages. There may be individual differences so far as the age of development is concerned but the sequence of development remains the same for all.

TABLE 7.1

Speech and Language Development at Different Ages (B.F. Skinner)

1. At birth language is practically absent.
2. At about 4 weeks small throaty sounds are noticed.
3. The starting point in language development is the child's cry or noise, smiles and cooing at the age of 16 weeks.
4. Around 28 weeks, the babbling stage begins. Now the baby makes sounds such as '*dadadada.*' The baby also vocalizes to toys. Initially the babbling sounds have no symbolic meaning. But the baby soon discovers that people, *dada* in the above instance, pay particular attention to him when he makes certain sounds. This reinforces the baby's sounds and he repeats these sounds.
5. Around 40 weeks, the baby imitates sounds made by adults and takes these sounds into his own system. Now the baby says one word.
6. Around 52 weeks, the baby says two or more words.
7. Around 18 months, the baby combines words to form basic sentence patterns.
8. Around 24 month, the baby uses simple phrases and understands simple directions.
9. Around 36 months, the child's vocabulary tremendously increases. Now he talks in sentences, and answers simple questions. The vocabulary explosion at 3 years occurs at about the same age in every healthy child throughout the world. It is at this age that some children are sent to the kindergarten, play group, day-care centres or preschool centres.
10. Around 4 years, the child uses conjunction and understands prepositions.
11. Around 5 years, the child speaks without infantile articulation. He asks "why?"
12. By their fifteenth birthday, almost all the normal children can speak and understand all kinds of sentences (such as simple, complex, active, passive, negative, interrogative, etc.) which any other adult speaker of their language is capable of using.

Source: Dash, M. & Dash Neena (2003). *Fundamentals of Educational Psychology*, New Delhi, Atlantic Publishers and Distributors, 104-105.

3. SYMPTOMS OF SPEECH HANDICAP

The symptoms of speech handicap are not general in nature. They are specific to the type of handicap. These various symptoms are as follows:

(i) Faulty pronunciation of words.

(ii) Variation in the pitch of the voice — too high or too low.

(iii) Stuttering and stammering while speaking.

(iv) Structural defect in the lips.

(v) Inability or difficulty in communicating ideas and feelings.

(vi) Trembling of voice.

(vii) Use of gestures and sign to communicate ideas.

(viii) Symptom of deafness.

4. CAUSES OF SPEECH HANDICAP

There is no specific cause of speech handicap. The factors which cause speech handicap may be physiological, environmental or mental:

(i) Loss of hearing, which may occur either from birth or due to accident, causes speech handicap. In any language learning, speaking always follows listening. In other words, the child must have the opportunity of listening others speaking in the language. A deaf child does not have the opportunity of hearing others and thus he is not able to speak. That is why a child is dumb largely because he is deaf.

(ii) Physiological defects in the lips and palate also cause speech handicap such as pronunciation disorder.

(iii) Cerebral palsy is another cause of speech handicap. Children suffering from cerebral palsy not only have speech handicap but also other disabilities like mental retardation.

(iv) Language and speech development depends upon mental development of the child. A child who has delayed mental development will have delayed speech development. The reason is that a child's mental development and his progress in speech development move along together.

(v) A child's speech development is influenced by the maturity of his vocal apparatus. If his vocal apparatus is not matured or defective it may cause speech handicap.

(vi) The family environment may also cause speech handicap. The parents provide the speech model to the child. If a child is deprived of this speech model he may not be able to speak correctly and develop speech handicap. If a child has developed stuttering or stammering and if parents make fun of his stuttering or stammering behaviour then that behaviour becomes serious and habitual.

(vii) In addition to these causes, extreme emotional disturbances in the child also cause speech handicap like stuttering and stammering. That is why emotionally disturbed children stutter or stammer more frequently than normal children.

5. PREVENTIVE MEASURES

The following preventive measures should be taken to prevent speech handicap:

(i) Speech handicap may occur if there is a cleft palate or structural defect in lips. A possible solution is surgical operation of the structural defect.

(ii) Young children imitate the sounds or speech patterns from elders. Hence elders must be very careful while talking to young children. If elders tend to stammer, may be out of making fun, while talking to young children they tend to imitate this speech pattern, and unless this is checked, it becomes a habit with them.

(iii) Tension provoking environments in the home and the school may lead to stammering and stuttering in children. Hence the home and the school environment must be tension-free.

(iv) Speech handicap also occurs due to faulty speech training by parents and teachers. Hence speech training must be free from errors.

(v) Young children naturally commit errors in speaking. But this should not be overemphasized by parents and teachers otherwise such overemphasis on speech defects may actually strengthen the defects.

(vi) Whenever a child is found to have speech defects careful and accurate diagnosis of the handicap should be made by speech therapist.

(vii) Whenever a child is found to have speech defect he should not be humiliated or put in an embarrassing situation in presence of his peers. If such care is not taken the child will hesitate or feel nervous to speak on future occasion for fear of committing mistakes in speech; he may remain dumb also.

6. EDUCATIONAL PROGRAMMES FOR SPEECH HANDICAPPED

Role of the Teacher

Speech handicapped children function normally in all situations excepting when oral communication is required. It is because of his deficiency in oral communication that his written expression is affected. The school curriculum is largely verbal in nature. The speech handicapped child has difficulty in school work largely because he has language handicap. The speech handicapped child should be given speech training, auditory training and language training so as to enable him to communicate and interact with others and make satisfactory progress in school work.

(i) *Speech Training and Auditory Training*

The speech handicapped child may have hearing problems. It is because he has not heard others speaking or because he is not able to hear properly, he is not able to speak correctly. Hence he should be given speech training and auditory training and this should start as early as possible in the home, preschool centres or speech clinics. (The reader is advised to refer to Chapter-6 on how to provide speech training and auditory training.)

(ii) *Language Training*

Speech handicapped children have delayed language

development. Thus they need language training. So far as the school is concerned such language training should begin in preschools. The following are some guidelines for language training in preschool years.

Listening with Attention

A major aspect of children's language development during preschool years and their language readiness for schools is attentive listening to conversation and other sounds around them. In a regular classroom children have to hear their teacher talk which takes at least 75 per cent of the class time. So classroom achievement depends largely on children's ability to listen and follow teacher's instruction. Children have to attend to only relevant and necessary sounds and talk, picking them up from a host of other noises. Thus, there has to be purposeful and attentive listening rather than simple indifferent hearing of sounds. The listening skills in preschool children have to be cultivated through a number of planned activities such as locating the source of a sound or imitation of various sounds, etc. Teacher's behaviour in preschools provides a model for children to follow. As such, the preschool teacher herself must listen to the children attentively in order to encourage attentive listening among them. If children are given instruction in preschools clearly but only once without any repetition as far as practicable, they will quickly learn not to miss the talk of the teacher and to attend to that carefully. But, the teacher may repeat an instruction if specifically requested by any child and while doing so, the teacher should also remind the children to be more careful in listening. It has, however, to be remembered that how much, at a time, preschool children can attend to and listen with comprehension has a limit and teacher's language use in preschool must be within the listening span of the children.

Provide Ample Opportunity for the Children to speak and to express

Often, adults and preschool teachers guess what a child wants to speak even before he expresses himself and act accordingly. As a result, the child is not encouraged to speak and to try to express himself. In order to foster expressive skills, the child has to be carefully and attentively heard without putting too much pressure on him to speak something often against his will. The preschool environment must be such that children feel quite relaxed and self-confident in expressing themselves.

Care in Correcting Mistakes in Children's Utterances

Mistakes and mispronunciation, stuttering, stammering, and hesitation are normal phenomena in children's language use during the preschool years and should be accepted as such. Creating much fuss over them and prompt correction particularly in front of others only serves to reduce children's motivation to express themselves in the language that the child acquires and the one he would be required to use in school. The situation is even more complicated for a large number of children for whom the school language is unrelated to the language they grow up with. In any case, children need to be prepared for school language use and the requirement for such preparation is even greater with children from lower socio-economic strata where the home language is much more different from the school language compared to such difference among the urban middle class children. To the extent that the primary objective of preschool training is to develop school readiness among 3 to 5 year old children, preschools must emphasize language training so that children can derive maximum benefit from regular schooling.

Language use in school is primarily a communication process and developing competence in such communicative arts has five aspects: (i) listening (with attentiveness), (ii) speaking, (iii) reading, (iv) writing and (v) use of language for abstract reasoning. It has been found that those children who have better competence in these aspects of communication arts are more successful in school compared to other children. Thus, to prepare children for high achievement in schools, preschool experience must focus on language training and on providing a rich linguistic environment for the child. Generally, some simple but basic rules have to be followed in preschools towards these objectives.

Talk to the Children in the Pre-schools

An important difference has been noticed between competent children who grow up to do well in schools and less competent ones who fail to profit from schooling. The mothers (as well as fathers and other adults) of competent children talk to their children more often than the mothers of the less competent ones.

In preschools also children need to be talked to. While talking to children *talk slowly, clearly and in simple sentences. Avoid baby talk with children.* The comprehension or understanding of any child or language user is always ahead of his own expressive capacity. So, although a child himself talks in a childlike manner, he is capable of understanding normal adult speech. If you talk to children as they talk to you, there is no propeller for furthering language growth which becomes slower, as a result.

Provide Language Experience through Stories and Songs

Stories and nursery rhymes are essential activities for enhancing children's expressive and receptive (understanding) skills. Children can be encouraged to tell a story from memory or to narrate a story from pictures. Children do not lose interest in a story told several times or singing a known song over and again. Rather, they find a known story or song more interesting than an unknown one. Telling stories from a book and allowing children to look in to the pictures in the book is an useful technique. Instead of direct and blunt correction, any error in their speech can be indirectly corrected by providing the correct form in subsequent conversation. Sometimes mistakes are natural course in language development and occur as a result of over-generalization of certain rules. For example, it is quite common among the English speaking children at a stage of their language development to say something like, "I goad there," as a result of over-generalization of the rule for past tense making. To point to the error, telling the children that they are wrong usually serves no purpose. The correct form ('went') can be given to the child by the teacher in his/her own conversation. Children need to hear a correct form several times before they begin to use it in their utterances. Telling the children, "don't say like this," only generates disinterestedness and result in a variety of speech disorders particularly in conditions of heightened emotionality such as anger and excitement.

With proper care and observance of these principles, it should not be difficult to accelerate adequate language development among pre-school children and to create readiness in them to meet the challenge of school language. With adequate receptive and expressive skills, transition to reading and writing instruction is not a problem. Reading readiness depends on communicative skills, knowledge of vocabulary and interest in books.

(iii) *Success Experience*

Speech handicapped children may have limitations in speech and language. But they may have strengths in other areas. For example, a speech handicapped child may be good in art, dance, and other co-curricular activities. He should be given the opportunity of participating in such activities and experiencing success. This gives him a sense of achievement and a feeling that he is an important member of the school community.

8

Orthopaedic Handicap

1. MEANING OF ORTHOPAEDIC HANDICAP

In our society we come across some children who are supposed to possess normal mental abilities but they are not able to maximize their potentialities due to one or the other type of physical handicap. These physically handicapped children are called differently by different authorities such as orthopaedically handicapped, crippled, children with locomotor handicap and children with neuromuscular disorder.

An orthopaedic handicap refers to defects in bones, muscles and joints. It is because of the defects (malformation or malfunction) in bones, muscles or joints the child is not able to use the limbs effectively. The child may feel pain in the joints. Such defects may interfere in his educational performance. The term 'crippled' refers to a kind of orthopaedic handicap in which the child's leg (or legs) is deformed or even the child loses his limbs and becomes lame.

The term loco-motor handicap also refers to a type of handicap in which the child's movements are affected because of disease or injury to the lower extremes of the body or nerves or spinal cord or because of loss of one leg or both legs.

Neuromuscular impairment refers to a specific impairment or dysfunction of the nervous system which adversely affects the education of the child.

Thus the term orthopaedic handicap covers all those conditions which prevent the child from having complete control of his bones, muscles, joints and the nervous system causing his inability to move about and/or use his limbs in a normal way. It includes polio effects, cerebral palsy, amputations resulting from accidents or disease, birth anomalies, muscular dystrophy and spina bifida.

2. SYMPTOMS OF ORTHOPAEDIC AND NEUROMUSCULAR HANDICAP

The symptoms of orthopaedic and neuromuscular handicap are as follows:

(i) Observable deformity in the child's limb — legs, arms, palms or feet (more than 40% as per report of the orthopaedician)

(ii) Awkward walking

(iii) Feeling of pain in the joints

(iv) Inabilities to use the bones and muscles

(v) Loss of any part of the body

(vi) Polio effects

(vii) Difficulty in bending the knees

(viii) Crippled body

(ix) Difficulty in walking/running some distance

(x) Abnormally short or weak hands or legs.

3. CAUSES OF ORTHOPAEDIC HANDICAP

There is no single cause of orthopaedic handicap. Rather it is caused by a number of factors which can be grouped under three heads such as:

(i) Hereditary,

(ii) Congenital and

(iii) Acquired or Environmental.

(i) Hereditary Factors

It is a fact that the physique of the child is inherited from parents. Even hereditary defects also pass down from one generation to another through genes. Some of the physical abnormalities which pass from one generation to another are: Claw hand, cleft palate, cleft lips, club foot, dislocation of hips, spina, bifida, etc.

(ii) Congenital Factors

Sometimes physical deformities occur due to congenital factors. In such cases the child is born with certain defects such as cleft lip, cleft palate, webbed fingers, club foot, bow leg, missing bones, etc. Some of the congenital factors are:

- Malnutrition of the pregnant mother;
- Infection and disease of the pregnant mother such as mumps, chicken pox, rubella, germane measles, Rh disease;
- High use of chemicals.

(iii) Environmental Factors

In addition to hereditary and congenital factors, environmental factors may also cause orthopaedic handicap. Some of these factors are as follows:

- Premature birth, long and difficult labour, caesarean birth hemorrhage and improper use of drugs may result in birth injuries.
- Infections and diseases such as whooping cough, measles, scarlet fever, tuberculosis of bones and joints and poliomyelitis, cerebral palsy, rheumatoid arthritis, leukaemia and blood cancer may also cause orthopaedic handicap.
- Lack of safety measures causing accidents.
- Nutritional deficiencies.
- War and natural calamities like earthquake, tsunami, etc.
- Lack of first aid for accident.
- Poverty of parents leading to lack of proper care and treatment for diseases.

4. PREVENTIVE MEASURES

The idea that prevention is better than cure holds true for orthopaedic handicap as for other disabilities.

(i) Prevention of orthopaedic impairment necessitates the concerted efforts of different professionals — physicians, nurses, social workers, volunteers, rehabilitation personnel.

(ii) Government and non-government organizations should work hand in hand to prevent the occurrence of orthopaedic handicaps.

(iii) Parents, particularly the pregnant mother should be educated through mass media and public awareness programmes about risk factors to be avoided so as to prevent the birth of an orthopaedic handicapped child or acquiring handicap after the birth.

(iv) Safety measures should be ensured in industries to prevent accidents.

(v) Safety education should be an integral part of school education.

(vi) Along with safety education, education about first aid and health education should also form an important part of the school education.

(vii) Community members should cooperate and participate in pulse polio programme and other mass immunization to prevent diseases which cause orthopaedic handicap.

(viii) Whenever the pregnant mothers or children are found to be suffering from diseases they should be treated immediately by competent physicians to avoid future handicaps that may result from such diseases.

(ix) Rehabilitation personnel have important role to play in the prevention of problems that may arise due to handicap. Orthopaedically handicapped persons should be suitably rehabilitated in the society and employments.

(x) Suitable aids and appliances should be made available to orthopaedically handicapped children to compensate for their disabilities. The Lions' club, the Rotary club, business firms and NGOs should come forward to provide aids and equipments to orthopaedically handicapped children free of cost.

5. EDUCATIONAL PROGRAMMES FOR ORTHOPAEDICALLY HANDICAPPED CHILDREN

Experts in the field of special education hold the view that orthopaedically handicapped children, particularly the crippled and others having mild to moderate degrees of handicap do not have learning problems. Like any other non-handicapped child an orthopaedically handicapped child can speak, read, write and solve arithmetic problems and make satisfactory progress in school work; he can have occupational success during adulthood; he can be an effective member of the community to which he belongs. But severely and profoundly handicapped children deprived of specialized training may have problems in these areas:

(i) The National Policy of Education (1986, Revised 1992) states "Wherever feasible education of children with locomotor handicaps...will be common with that of others." Thus, orthopaedically handicapped children should be educated in regular schools. This is not only feasible, it is also cost effective.

(ii) Most of these children are already in the regular schools. They need to be identified early so that interventions can be initiated by the schools.

(iii) Education of orthopaedically handicapped children in regular schools necessitates removal of architectural barriers in the schools. Because these children have problems of movement and some of them may use wheel-chair and crutches, barriers to their movement such as staircase should be removed and alternate arrangements should be made for them. If possible their classrooms may be located in the ground floor of the building.

(iv) For successful education these children may require aids and equipments. The school must arrange to provide aids and equipments from various sources for such children. A child with impairments in the waist, hips and joint pains requires furniture which can be adjusted to his needs. A child having loss of fingers or defective fingers requires special writing materials such as thick pen. A child with a missing limb requires artificial limb. Crippled children may require wheel-chair and crutches. The Rotary Cub, Lions' Club and NIRTAR may be approached for this purpose.

(v) The school should give opportunity to the orthopaedically handicapped to participate in co-curricular activities keeping in view their difficulties and potentialities. Wherever possible handicapped and non-handicapped children should be involved in the same activities. This will develop in them friendship and mutual appreciation.

(vi) The most important thing is teacher's acceptance and attitude towards orthopaedically handicapped children. Orthopaedically handicapped children should be accepted by teachers as equal members of the school community. The favourable attitude of teachers will develop among peers a favorable attitude towards orthopaedically handicapped child.

(vii) The individuality and diversity of such children should be valued by teachers and opportunity should be made available to them to experience success in academic and co-academic programmes.

(viii) In all cases teachers should avoid labeling such children as 'lame', 'crippled', etc. Labeling has adverse effects on psycho-social aspect of their development.

9

Severe and Multiple Handicap

1. WHAT IS MULTIPLE HANDICAP?

Multiple handicaps refer to presence of more than one handicap in the individual. Thus when an individual suffers from more than one handicap he is called multiple handicapped. For example an individual may be blind and deaf. Neither he can see nor can he hear. Similarly an individual may be blind and orthopaedically handicapped. A child may have cerebral palsy and mental retardation. When an individual has multiple handicaps one handicap may be the primary handicap and the other secondary. For example, in a child who is both blind and deaf loss of vision may be the primary handicap. Loss of hearing becomes the secondary handicap for him or the *vice versa*. Helen Keller was multiple handicapped. She was both blind and deaf. But the occurrence of multiple handicaps is very less in the population as compared to the occurrence of single handicap.

Usually multiple handicapped individuals are severely handicapped and that is why we talk about "severe and multiple handicap."

2. SYMPTOMS OF MULTIPLE HANDICAP

It is difficult to pinpoint the general symptoms of multiple handicaps. The symptoms of multiple handicaps depend upon the combination of handicaps which make an individual multiple handicapped. If an individual has loss of vision along with loss of hearing his symptoms will be almost like those of a visually impaired and hearing impaired individual. In that case the dominant symptoms will depend upon his primary handicap. It is important that we must understand the primary handicap of a multiple handicapped child which will be evident from his dominant symptoms. Other symptoms will indicate his secondary handicap.

3. CAUSES OF MULTIPLE HANDICAP

Multiple handicaps may occur from birth. Multiple handicaps which occur from birth pose severe problems for the individual. Sometimes an individual may have one handicap from birth. But due to environmental factors such as disease, accident or injury he may become handicapped in another aspect. For example a child may be born with hearing impairment and due to poisonous substances or due to accident he may loose his eye sight and becomes multiple handicapped. The same factors which make a child handicapped in vision, hearing or movement may also cause multiple handicap.

4. IDENTIFICATION OF MULTIPLE HANDICAPS

Identification of multiple handicaps should always be made by competent and trained specialist doctors. Before this is done parents and teachers can detect multiple handicap in a child based on the problems and complaints of the child. The following techniques can be used:

(i) Day-to-day observation of the problems experienced by the child.

(ii) Child's complaints about his difficulties.

(iii) Report by siblings in the home.

(iv) Behavioural characteristics.

(v) Child's performance on assignments/tasks.

If a child is found to have problems in at least two dimensions — vision, hearing, speech, loco-motor movement, intellectual functioning, etc. he should be immediately referred to specialist doctor for thorough investigation and medical assessment. If necessary psychological assessment may be also made.

5. CHARACTERISTICS OF MULTIPLE HANDICAPPED

The characteristics of multiple handicapped children vary from child to child depending upon the specific handicapping conditions. However the following generalizations about the characteristics of multiple handicapped children can be made:

(i) *Self-concept* — Multiple handicapped children have a poor self concept. This is the most severely affected aspect of the child's development.

(ii) *Language and speech* — The language and speech development of the multiple handicapped child, particularly if he is both blind and deaf or deaf and dumb is impaired.

(iii) *Intellectual functioning* — Intellectual functioning of multiple handicapped child is much below average.

(iv) *Social adjustment* — These children have difficulty in personal-social adjustment.

(v) *Social interaction* — These children are, most often, not liked by their peers. Hence they have few friends. Some of them are isolated in the circle of peers.

(vi) *Educational perspective* — In view of their multiple handicaps these children are hard cases for education in school. It is for this reason, teachers do not enroll such children in school. However, whatever little success is possible it depends entirely on superior instruction and constant care.

6. PREVENTIVE MEASURES

Preventive measures aim at preventing the problems of multiple handicapped children from becoming serious ones. Most multiple handicapped children live a miserable life because of lack of proper care, training and understanding. Parents have major role to play to help such children live better and feel secure:

(i) Multiple handicapped children are like any other non-handicapped children excepting their handicapping conditions. But they do not need mercy from others. Like any other child in the family they have a right to live, work and to be taken care of. Such children should be granted their basic rights.

(ii) Parents need to deal with the problems of such children with a sympathetic understanding.

(iii) Instead of rejecting such children parents should treat them with equality. Such children should be given such responsibilities in the home which they can discharge successfully. They must feel they are important members in the family.

(iv) Whenever a child is found to have multiple handicaps he must be given proper care — medical care and parental care. Intensive and constant care by parents can alleviate most of their problem.

(v) Superior instruction by parents and private tutors can help them to learn the essential skills required for independent living in the community. Hellen Keller could learn language because of intensive care by her parents and superior instruction by her private tutor.

(vi) Lack of acceptance and unfavourable attitude of parents are the greatest barriers for the development and welfare of such children. Hence these children must be accepted by parents and other members of the family. Everyone in the family should show positive attitude towards such children.

(vii) Some multiple handicapped children may have the potential for learning in special schools and residential schools. Whenever possible attempts should be made to educate them in special schools and residential schools. Their education should emphasize basic academic skills, civic efficiency, self care skills and economic independence.

(viii) Concerted efforts of social worker, special educators, physicians and rehabilitation personnel are required for the welfare of handicapped children.

10

Delinquency

1. MEANING OF DELINQUENCY

Delinquency is a social problem which is increasing day by day and has become the concern for parents, teachers and community members. What is delinquency?

Delinquency is a term which is easy to explain than to define it. It is a term that stands for a number of anti-social behaviours. Its meaning varies from time to time, society to society and culture to culture. Thus it is a culture-specific term. What is considered as a delinquent act in Indian culture may be accepted as normal in western culture.

Every society lays down certain moral code of conduct, rules and regulations for its members. It is also expected that every member will abide by these code of conduct, rules and regulations laid down by the society. Every society has also passed laws for punishing individuals who violate these rules and regulations and the code of conduct. They are viewed as anti-socials or criminals in the eyes of laws. If such anti-social behaviours and crimes are noticed among teen-agers or young men and women below the age of 16 or 18 these are called delinquent acts or delinquency. In our country any teen-age who is found to be indulged in anti-social acts which are punishable under the existing law is called a juvenile delinquent and his anti-social acts are called juvenile offences. Therefore, juvenile delinquents are criminals minor in age or "minors with major social problems".

2. DEFINITION OF DELINQUENCY

Delinquency is such a complex behavioural tendency that there is no unanimity among professionals regarding its definition. Different professionals have defined delinquency differently depending upon what they believe to be the central factor in such antisocial acts. Some have defined the term in terms of faulty personality development. Similarly some definitions relate to the mode of expression of needs, desires and drives. It is significant here to quote some of the definitions:

"The delinquent is an individual in whom instructive drives are strong, conscience is weak, and the ego is based upon immediate pleasure without respect to the generally accepted norms of behaviour." — Coll

"Delinquency refers to holes in the superego." — Johnson and Szurek

"Delinquency means moral deficiency because of weak conscience due to improper teaching of the children in early years of life." — Mowrer

There is one thing common in all the above three definitions — delinquency is the manifestation of weak superego in the individual. Superego acts as the conscience of the individual. When an individual's superego is not developed properly he cannot distinguish between good and evil, between what is desirable or acceptable behaviour and what is undesirable or unacceptable behaviour. In such circumstance the id in the individual which is guided by the pleasure principle dominates the super ego. The id desires influence the individual to commit anti-social acts and we call it delinquency, (For more information about id, ego and super ego readers may refer to the author's book *Fundamentals of Educational Psychology*, 25-26).

Some professionals define delinquencies in terms of frustrations in life. Look at these definitions:

"Juvenile delinquents are persons who habitually respond to serious and prolonged frustration in aggressive ways." — Plant

"Delinquency is the manifestation of frustrated needs of the child which ultimately lead to aggression." — Bandura and Walter

"Delinquency is the result of unsuccessful efforts to achieve goals legitimately thereby causing the individual to engage in antisocial, non legal avenues to obtain material wealth and social status." — Merton

Every individual has certain needs. Satisfaction of these needs becomes the goal before him. When he fails to satisfy his needs and reach his goal by socially accepted means because of his personal inadequacy or socio-economic factors he tries to reach his goal by anti-social activities and we call it delinquency.

Most often delinquency is defined in terms of offences committed which are punishable under law. The following definitions are worth-noting:

"The delinquent is a person whose misbehavior is relatively serious legal offence, which is inappropriate to his level of development, is not committed as a result of extremely low intellect and is not alien to the culture in which he has been reared." — Herbert Quay

"Juvenile delinquency is defined as the violation of a law that, if committed by an adult, would be a crime." — Skinner

"Delinquency is defined by acts, the detection of which is thought to result in punishment of the person committing them by agents of the larger society." — Travis Hirchi

"A child is to be regarded as technically delinquent when his antisocial tendencies appear so grave that he becomes or ought to become the subject of official action." — Cyril Burt

"A delinquent is a child or youth, who repeatedly commits acts which are punishable as crimes." — Klausmeier and Goodwin

Certain facts emerge from these definitions:

(i) Delinquent acts are like criminal acts

(ii) Since these anti-social activities are committed by youth or children below 18 years these acts are called juvenile offences

(iii) If these offences occur repeatedly and are of serious nature they are punishable as per the law of the society

(iv) Delinquent acts are not committed out of ignorance of social rules or because of low intelligence. These acts are intentional and hence can be regarded as immoral.

Types of Delinquent Acts

Interpretation of acts as delinquent acts varies from culture to culture. So far as the Indian culture is concerned, the following acts are considered as delinquent acts:

(i) Damaging school property

(ii) Truancy from school

(iii) Obscene drawing and writing on the school wall, and in classrooms

(iv) Obscene talks

(v) Making sexual appeals to girls

(vi) Stealing books, pens, money from peers' school bags

(vii) Forgery of parents' signature in progress cards and check books

(viii) Committing suicide

(ix) Homo-sexuality

(x) Sexual contacts with girls and women

(xi) Raping

(xii) Teasing and bullying.

3. BEHAVIORAL CHARACTERISTICS OF DELINQUENTS

Delinquent children and youth are often classified into two groups depending upon their behavioural and physical characteristics.

First Group of Delinquents

(i) They are mesomorphic in constitution, muscular and bold.

(ii) They love physical adventure and enjoyment.

(iii) They love taking risk and chance.

(iv) They are very direct in their manner.

(v) If necessary they are ready for fights.

(vi) They are restlessly energetic.

(vii) They are impulsive in nature.

(viii) They are extroverted.

(ix) They are aggressive and destructive.

(x) They are hostile, and resentful.

(xi) They are defiant. They defy school rules and discipline.

(xii) They hate school, criticize teachers and like to roam about. They run away from the school. They are truants.

(xiii) They are less submissive to authorities. They may prefer to leave the school rather than to submit to the authority.

Truancy, destruction of school property, attacking teachers, quarrelling and fighting with peers, teasing and bullying girls, sexual appeals to girls and even raping, etc. may be found among such delinquents.

Second Group of Delinquents

(i) They are asthenic in body build, thin or weak

(ii) They may be pessimistic, suspicious and depressed

(iii) They are shy, quiet and introverted

(iv) They may be selfish

(v) They are vindictive in nature

(vi) They lack in feelings of shame

(vii) They may pose a smiling face but internally they are of hard nature

Stealing pen, book or money from peers' bags, writing love letters secretly to girls, obscene drawings and writing in the school walls, forgery of signature, committing suicide, etc. may be found among this group of delinquents.

4. IDENTIFICATION AND ASSESSMENT

Delinquent children should be identified early and assessed properly so that intervention measures can be initiated to reduce their anti-social activities or eliminate such activities completely. The following techniques and tools can be used to identify delinquent children:

(i) Day-to-day observation of children's behaviour and interaction with peers, teachers and authority

(ii) Report of peers about the child's activities during the school hour and beyond school hour

(iii) Report of parents about their child

(iv) Report of community leaders about the child

(v) Check list for teachers to indicate the child's conduct, temperaments and attitude

(vi) Rating scale for teachers' judgment about the child

(vii) School records such as cumulative record card, attendance register, notices to parents, fines imposed on the child, applications and undertaking given by the child/parents, etc.

(viii) Interview schedule for obtaining pertinent information about the child and his home environment/background.

These techniques will provide information about the anti-social activities committed by the child, frequency of such activities and the seriousness of such activities. Delinquents thus identified should be referred to psychologists and psychiatrists who will conduct counseling session, administer psychological tests and psychotherapy to make accurate judgment about such children and help parents and teachers to bring about reformation in their behaviour, temperaments, attitudes and conduct.

5. EDUCATIONAL STRATEGIES

Educational strategies to deal with delinquents imply two strategies — Prevention of delinquency and Treatment of delinquent children.

Prevention of Delinquency

Prevention is better than cure, Preventive measures aim at checking the occurrence of delinquency among children and youth in future. It involves the coordinated efforts of parents, teachers and community members. The following guidelines may serve the purpose of preventing the occurrence of delinquency:

(i) The home environment is a major cause of children developing delinquent tendencies. Relationship between the father and the mother — divorce, separation and frequent quarrel in presence of the child — has adverse effect on the mental heath of the child. Loving relationship among parents and a tension free home environment can ensure prevention of delinquent tendencies among children.

(ii) Relationship between parents and the child is also a significant cause of delinquency. Children who are unwanted in the home, children who are rejected by parents, children who are deprived of the love and affection of parents, and children who are overprotected or underprotected develop delinquent tendencies. Hence the relationship between parents and the child should be cordial, pleasant and one that is based on mutual trust, understanding and respect.

(iii) Children become delinquents largely due to lack of proper guidance and teaching by parents. Parents should therefore develop good habits, attitude and value systems among their children. Moral education should form an important aspect of the home curriculum.

In our society most of the parents are illiterate or half-educated. Hence they should be educated about child rearing practices, parents-child relationship, etc. in the meeting of parent-teacher association.

(iv) Parents should arrange to provide recreational activities and literature based on moral values for their children. They should understand the growing needs of their adolescent sons and daughters and try to meet their needs as far as possible.

(v) Children should be advised properly and protected from interacting with anti-social elements in the community.

(vi) The atmosphere of the school should be free from emotional tension arising out of stress and conflict.

(vii) There should be adequate provisions for co-curricular

activities in the school so that children and adolescents can release their pent-up energies.

(viii) There should be healthy interpersonal relationship among students, between students and teachers and among teachers.

(ix) Teachers should behave with students as father figures.

(x) Every child should be treated with equality. Every child should have opportunity for experiencing success depending upon his needs, interests and abilities.

Treatment and Educational Programme

Delinquent youth can be treated by applying the techniques of psychotherapy. The psychotherapist observes the delinquent youth and studies the magnitude of his problems. He plays the role of a counselor and treats the counselee by applying any one of the six techniques mentioned below:

(i) Reeducation which aims at reeducating the delinquent about desirable behaviours and clarifying his ideas on different problems he faces in his life.

(ii) Abreaction which aims at providing opportunity to the delinquent to express his pent-up and suppressed emotional feelings by means of discussion, free association, free expression etc.

(iii) Persuasion which aims at appealing to the conscience of the delinquent and persuading him not to indulge in anti-social activities in future.

(iv) Suggestion and counseling which aim at giving positive suggestion to strengthen his super ego.

(v) Environmental treatment which aims at advising parents to improve their relations, attitude and behaviour towards the delinquent child and to take him to a new environment for a temporary period to start a new life afresh.

(vi) Behaviour modification which is based on the notion that anti-social behaviour has been learned and that desirable behaviour can also be learnt following the Skinnerian principles of reinforcement.

In addition to these therapeutic measures the school has also an important role to play:

(i) The school curriculum should be meaningful to children.

(ii) It should have relevance to the life and needs of those passing out from the school.

(iii) School education should be productivity-oriented and develop in students the knowledge, skills and competencies for their economic independence.

(iv) Moral and spiritual education should be an integral part of education right from the primary level.

(v) Facilities should be available in all schools for participation in games and sports and other co-curricular activities.

(vi) There should be healthy interaction between teachers and students based on mutual trust and understanding.

(vii) The classroom transaction should be as enjoyable as possible.

(viii) Behaviour problems that may occur in the classroom and the school should be solved amicably with an understanding attitude.

(ix) The school discipline should be made known to everybody right from the day of admission and everybody should be advised to abide by these disciplinary rules.

(x) Guidance services, particularly personal guidance services, should be organized in secondary schools. An experienced teacher of the school should remain in charge of such guidance and counseling services.

11

Gifted and Slow Learners

A. GIFTED CHILDREN

1. Who are the Gifted?

There is no unanimous agreement about the definition of giftedness. The profusion of definitions of giftedness is great which is probably due to the fact there are many kinds of gifted children. Moreover, each culture defines giftedness in its own image, in terms of the abilities that the culture values. For example, ancient Greeks honoured the philosopher and the orator and Romans valued the engineer and the soldier.

Giftedness has been traditionally associated with intellectual superiority — a very high IQ score on a standardized test of intelligence. Over the past few decades, periodic efforts have been made to broaden the definition of giftedness to include more than abilities directly related to school work. As for instance, Maryland (1972) defined gifted students as follows: "Gifted and talented children are those, identified by professionally qualified persons, who, by virtue of outstanding abilities, are capable of high performance." These are children who require differentiated programmes and services beyond those normally provided by the regular school programmes in order to realize their contributions to self and society. Adolescents capable of high performance include those with demonstrated achievement and/or potential ability in any one of the following areas:

(i) General intellectual ability

(ii) Specific academic aptitude

(iii) Creative or productive thinking
(iv) Leadership ability
(v) Visual and performing arts.

One of the latest definitions of giftedness has been given by Ross (1993). According to Ross, "Children and youth with outstanding talent perform, or show the potential for performing, at reasonably high levels of accomplishments when compared with others of their age, experience, or environment. These children and youth exhibit high performance capability in intellectual, creative and/or artistic areas, possess an unusual leadership capacity or excel in specific academic fields. They require services or activities not ordinarily provided by the schools. Outstanding talents are present in children and youth from all cultural groups, across all economic strata, and in all areas of human endeavour."

Other definitions of giftedness try to include the way an individual defines and then tackles a problem — the ability to *problem-find* and *problem-solve*. In the real world, problems do not come in neat packages ready for solving. Usually they are hard to define and organise. Problems in the real world are ill-structured. The ability to take an ill-structured problem and organise it so that the issue is clear is one indicator of giftedness. Thus, "Gifted students are those who demonstrate or show the potential for outstanding performance in academic, creative, artistic, leadership or problem-solving areas and who require special education and related services to actualize their potentialities and maximize their capacities."

2. Identification of Gifted Children

Our society has a special interest in children who are gifted. As individuals they have the same right to appropriate education as do all children. In addition, many of the leaders, scientists, engineers and doctors of the twentieth century came from the current group of gifted children. This necessitates early identification of gifted children and provision of suitable education and other services for them.

Gifted adolescents are usually identified by subjective and objective methods, such as the following:

Intelligence Scores
Creativity Measures
Achievement Measures
Measures of Special Aptitude (such as in Mathematics)
Nomination of Peers
Nomination by Parents
Self-Nomination.

It is important to note that no single method can identify all gifted and talented children. A combination of subjective and objective methods is desirable for identifying gifted and talented children.

Identification Checklist for Parents: Parents can identify their gifted children before they enter the primary school with the help of the following checklist as suggested by Witty (1955). Such identification/nomination by parents should be followed by systematic assessment by specialists:

(i) The early use of a large and accurately employed vocabulary.
(ii) The use of entire sentences and ability to tell or reproduce a story at an early date.
(iii) Keen observation and retention of information about things observed.
(iv) Interest in and liking for books.
(v) Early interest in calendars, telling time, and clocks.
(vi) The ability to attend or concentrate for a longer period than is usual for children.
(vii) Demonstration of proficiency in drawing, music, or other art form.
(viii) Interest in exploration and discovery of cause and effect relationships.
(ix) The early development of ability to read.

Identification Checklist for Teachers: The classroom teacher has the primary responsibility of identifying the gifted adolescents. He is in a better position than anyone else to observe the classroom behaviour of adolescents. In order to make the teacher's observation/nomination more systematic, Koogh and De Haan (1955) have suggested the following checklist:

(i) Learns rapidly and easily.

(ii) Uses a lot of common sense and practical knowledge.

(iii) Reasons things out, thinks clearly, recognizes relationships and comprehends meanings.

(iv) Retains what he has heard or read without much drill.

(v) Knows about many things of which other children are unaware.

(vi) Can read books that are one to two years in advance of the rest of the class.

(vii) Performs difficult mental tasks.

(viii) Asks many questions.

(ix) Does some academic work one to two years in advance of the rest of the class.

(x) Is original, uses good but unusual methods or ideas.

(xi) Is alert, keenly observant and responds quickly.

It is important to note that nomination by a group of teachers is more valid than nomination by a single teacher. In any case identification/nomination by teachers should be followed by objective methods of identification and assessment by specialists.

3. Characteristics of Gifted Children

Giftedness is a complex concept covering a wide range of abilities and traits. Some children have special talents. They may not be outstanding in academics, but they may have special abilities in areas such as music, art, dance, or leadership. Other children may have intellectual abilities found only in one child out of 1,000 children.

Clark (1988) describes the characteristics of gifted children across five domains: cognitive, affective, physical, intuitive, and societal. There are individual differences among gifted children relating to these characteristics. These characteristics are given below:

I. The Cognitive Domain

- Extraordinary quantity of information; unusual retentiveness
- Advanced comprehension
- Unusually varied interests and curiosity
- High level of language development
- High level of verbal ability
- Unusual capacity for processing information
- Accelerated pace of thought process
- Flexible thought process
- Comprehensive synthesis
- Early ability to delay closure
- Heightened capacity for seeing unusual and diverse relationships and overall gestalt
- Ability to generate original ideas and solutions
- Early differential patterns for thought processing (*e.g.* thinking in alternatives and abstract terms, sensing consequences, making generalizations)
- Early ability to use and form conceptual frameworks
- An evaluative approach toward oneself and others
- Persistent goal-directed behaviour

II. The Affective Domain

- Large accumulation of information about emotions that have not been brought to awareness
- Unusual sensitivity to the expectations and feelings of others
- Keen sense of humour — may be gentle or hostile
- Heightened self-awareness, accompanied by feelings of being "different"
- Idealism and a sense of justice that appear at an early age
- Earlier development of an inner locus of control and satisfaction

- Advanced level on moral judgment
- High expectations of self and others, which often lead to high levels of frustration with self, others, and situations
- Unusual emotional depth and intensity
- Sensitivity to inconsistency between ideals and behaviour.

III. The Physical Domain

- Unusual discrepancy between physical and intellectual development
- Low tolerance for the lag between their standards and their physical capacity
- Cartesian split — can include neglect of physical well-being and avoidance of physical activity.

IV. The Intuitive Domain

- Early involvement and concern for intuitive knowing, psychic and metaphysical phenomena
- Open to experiences in this area; will experiment with and metaphysical phenomena
- Creativity apparent in all areas of endeavour
- Acceptance and expression of a high level of intuitive ability, especially with the highly gifted.

V. The Societal Domain

- Strongly motivated by self-actualization needs
- Advanced cognitive and affective capacity for conceptualizing and solving societal problems.

4. Underachieving Gifted Adolescents

Some adolescents with superior intellectual ability don't perform well in the school. Some gifted students actually fail in the school. In such cases, there is a discrepancy between their potentialities and their actual performance. They are called the underachieving gifted adolescents.

Terman and Oden (1947) found four major factors of underachievement of gifted students:

(i) Greater feelings of inferiority
(ii) Less self-confidence
(iii) Less perseverance
(iv) Less of a sense of life goals.

Gowan (1987) has summarized the research findings and concluded that the following factors are related to underachievement:

(i) Lack of clear and definite academic and occupational choice
(ii) Weak ego control
(iii) Withdrawal tendency and feelings of self-sufficiency
(iv) Poor use of time and money
(v) Neurotic tendencies
(vi) Authoritarianism by parents
(vii) Impossible demands by parents
(viii) A sense of irresponsibility
(ix) Lack of self-confidence
(x) Apathetic view of life.

Gallagher (1960) presents a combination of events which lead to underachievement among children of superior intelligence:

(i) The underachieving child grows up in, or belongs to, a cultural group which does not value education, independence or individual achievement.
(ii) The underachieving child has parents (especially the father) who show limited interest in academic matters or try to put undue pressure on their children to succeed.
(iii) Faced with impossible demands by parents in home and teachers in the school, the child rejects their programmes.
(iv) The strict and repressive measures of the school turn the child even more emphatically against the school.
(v) Unable to obtain satisfaction from parental contacts, the child seeks out his peer group for satisfying human

relationships. He often finds himself in rebellious and angry groups.

Whitmore (1980) found the following personality and behaviour traits that describe many underachieving gifted children:

(i) A negative self-concept
(ii) A low self-esteem
(iii) Expectation of academic and social failure
(iv) A sense of inability to control or determine outcomes of one's own efforts
(v) Emotional disturbance.

Most of the factors that lead to underachievement lie outside the school. What can the school do to help the underachieving gifted child? Kirk (1972) suggests the following measures:

(i) Identifying underachieving gifted children during the early years in school.
(ii) Assigning tutors who will support and motivate the children through success in academic fields.
(iii) Counselling parents concerning the problems of the child and better human relations in the family.
(iv) Rewarding the child by praise and recognition in school for efforts and achievements in school work.
(v) Organising small group sessions/special classes for underachieving gifted children with support from specialist teachers.

Whitmore (1980) points out that the creation of a warm, accepting environment can overcome the signs of emotional disturbance of such children. Whitmore (1980) and Butler-Por (1987) have shown that carefully designed programmes over an extended period of time can make a positive difference in the academic and social performance of underachievers.

5. Educational Programmes for the Gifted Children

Aims of Education of the Gifted: In a broader sense, the aims of education of the gifted are no different from those for all other children. Feelings of self-worth, self-sufficiency, civic responsibilities, and vocational competence are important for everyone. There are, however, some additional goals which are specially desirable for gifted and talented children. Gallagher (1981) has suggested two major objectives of educational programmes for the gifted and talented children:

(i) Mastering the knowledge structure of disciplines which includes basic principles and systems of knowledge.

(ii) Heuristic skills which include problem-solving, creativity, and use of the scientific methods.

Setting educational goals for gifted children means little unless these children are given appropriate learning opportunities, or unless the school programmes are modified to match their special needs. The school programme for the gifted can be modified in three areas: learning environments, content, and cognitive strategies (Kirk, Gallagher and Anastasiow, 1996).

Modification in the Learning Environment: The learning environment can be modified for the gifted and talented students in three ways. These are:

(i) Flexible pacing

(ii) Grouping and

(iii) Special courses.

(i) *Flexible Pacing:* Flexible pacing is a strategy that accelerates the student to a level in the school programme that is higher than the level of his/her age-mates. This strategy involves the following:

- Early admission in the school or college
- Continuous progress at one's own rate
- Skipping (bypassing) subjects and receiving some instruction at a higher level with another group of students while remaining with the peer group for most of the instruction
- Skipping grades (double promotion)
- Concurrent (dual) enrolment at two levels — secondary and post-secondary

- Giving credit on satisfactory completion of an examination
- Covering the course in a shortened period of time and pursuing special courses during the rest of the time.

(ii) *Grouping:* Students can be grouped on the basis of performance or aptitude. Having all students with high performance ability in one group allows the teacher to proceed much more swiftly and in greater depth. Grouping can be of various types:

- Cross-age or multi-age grouping of students on the basis of similar interests or skills.
- Homogenous grouping of students in a particular class on the basis of similar skill level.
- Cluster grouping within a regular class in which a cluster group (4 to 10) of students receives academic support from the cluster teacher.
- Subject grouping in which students are grouped for specific subjects on the basis of their performance or aptitude in that subject.
- Part-time placement in the regular class with part-time placement in a special class for specialized instruction.
- Full-time placement in a special class.

(iii) *Special Courses:* At the secondary level, special courses can be organised for gifted and talented students. These include:

- Honours courses
- Advanced placement courses or college-level courses
- International courses and foreign languages
- Special school courses
- Residential high school courses not available in most high schools.

Modification of Content. Boredom is a real problem for gifted students because they are forced to learn material they already know. For this reason, the teacher needs to:

- Find out what the students know before instruction,

- Arrange to teach, in a brief fashion, the remaining concepts or skills and
- Provide a different set of experiences to enrich or advance the students.

Content modification involves the following:

Content acceleration,

Content enrichment,

Content sophistication and

Content novelty.

(i) *Content Acceleration:* This process allows students to master increasingly complex set of ideas at a faster rate. For example, by learning calculus in ninth grade, students have the foundation to begin physics and chemistry which require the skills of calculus.

(ii) *Content Enrichment:* This process gives students the opportunity for a greater appreciation of the topic under study by expanding the material — exploring additional examples, using specific illustration, taking additional assignments, referring to encyclopaedia, etc.

(iii) *Content Sophistication:* This process involves challenging students who are gifted to use higher levels of thinking to understand ideas that average students of the same age would find difficult or impossible to comprehend. The objective is to encourage gifted children to understand important abstractions, scientific laws, and general principles that can be applied in many circumstances.

(iv) *Content Novelty:* Content novelty is the introduction of material that normally would not appear in the general curriculum because of time constraints or the abstract nature of the content. Computers can be used to introduce content novelty into the curriculum.

Teaching Cognitive Strategies. One objective of all educators of gifted and talented students is to increase or enhance their capability in problem-finding and problem-solving. Problem-finding is the ability to review an area of study and to perceive those elements worthy of further analysis and study. Problem-solving is the ability to reach a previously determined answer by organising and processing the available information in a logical and systematic fashion. Along with enhancing their problem-finding and problem-solving skills, gifted and talented students should be guided to extend their intellectual fluency through *brainstorming*. The four ground rules for brainstorming are as follows:

(i) No criticism should be allowed when a student presents an idea.

(ii) The more ideas, the better.

(iii) Students should be encouraged to integrate and combine ideas.

(iv) Evaluation should take place after all ideas have been presented.

6. Role of the Teacher

No educational programme is more important than the teacher who implements it. Most schools do not get the services of a specialist teacher for educating gifted and talented students. Hence, the regular teacher has to play an important role in identifying children who are gifted, assessing their potentialities, modifying the learning environment, providing acceleration and enrichment and organise brainstorming sessions for gifted students.

One of the first questions most people ask is whether the teacher must be gifted to teach gifted children effectively. The answer is "Not necessarily." In fact, all teachers must be gifted, regardless of whom they teach. They should be gifted in different ways to teach different children. Nonetheless, teachers of gifted children do need some particular qualities. They must:

- be willing to accept unusual and diverse questions, answers and projects;
- be intellectually curious;
- be systematic and business-like;
- be well prepared in instructional techniques;

- be well prepared in content areas;
- have a variety of interests;
- appreciate achievements;
- realize that they may not know as much about some topics as the children, and be comfortable with that situation (Heward and Orlansky, 1992).

B. SLOW LEARNERS

1. Who is a Slow Learner?

It is a known fact that all children experience school-related problems at one time or another during their school years. A teacher on any working day may have to deal with problems ranging from aggressive behaviour to disinterest in the learning task. The cause of such difficulties may vary from an unknown conflict at home to simple headache. Such situations may result in poor academic performance and aggressive behaviour temporarily. Effective teachers tackle such problems easily. There is, however, another group of children who display prolonged learning difficulties. These are the children whose scholastic performance is below the average expected of their age-group. Most teachers who deal with average and below-average pupils meet children who do not seem to profit from the usual educational methods and content provided. The term 'backward' or 'slow learner' is reserved for these children who are not coping with the work normally expected of their age group (Burt, 1937) or whose scholastic performance is below the average expected of their age group (Kirman, 1975).

For Kirk (1962), rate of learning is the basis of identifying a child as slow learner, average or gifted. For Kirk, the slow-learning child is not considered mentally retarded because he is capable of achieving a moderate degree of academic success even though at a slower rate than the average child. He is educated in the regular classes without special provisions except an adaptation of the regular class programme to fit his slower learning ability. At the adult level, he is usually self-supporting, independent and socially adjusted.

There are some children who have borderline retardation and some who have mild retardation. Individuals with borderline mental retardation blend with the normal population, and with proper training can achieve social and vocational adequacy. This group and those mild mental retardates who remain undetected in a class are often called 'slow learners.' The child we call a slow learner is one who is not necessarily retarded or in need of special education but is likely to need some extra time and help in a regular classroom. He is capable of learning just about anything that the average child is capable of; it just takes him longer. In other words, a slow learner is one who learns or is learning at a slower than average rate.

2. Causes of Slow Learning

Every behaviour has a cause, meaning and significance. The behavioural characteristics of slow learners are symptoms of conditions or some factors present either within the child or outside the child. Slow learning is caused by a variety of factors such as:

(i) Low intellectual abilities such as subnormal intelligence.

(ii) Personal factors such as:
long illness,
long absence from school,
undetected physical defects,
poor cognitive entry characteristics.

(iii) Environmental variables such as:
poor home facilities for learning skills,
low quality and quantity of food,
shortage of sleep,
adverse parental attitudes towards education,
poor or inappropriate opportunities in school (large classes),
poor quality of teaching,
choosing inadequate or advanced materials,
incompatibility between home and the school,
repeated changes of school and consequent changes in teaching styles and content.

(iv) Emotional factors such as:
dislike of teacher through classes of personality,
negative parental attitudes to school creating in the child similar adverse attitudes,
feeling of inadequacy,
lack of confidence in self and need to achieve,
extreme timidity and anxiety giving rise to poor levels of attainment.

3. Identification of Slow Learners

In every classroom, a large number of slow learners are noticed. These children with borderline or mild handicaps who attend the regular class are likely to drop out if their needs are not met. It is, therefore, necessary that these children are identified early and helped in their learning. A competent teacher should be alert to general characteristics of the associated classroom behaviour relating to learning difficulties of a child. For example, the slow learner requires more help and time to acquire the skill than his average peer. The slow learner will rely on concrete learning rather than abstract learning.

Slow learners are to be identified by employing various procedures and using various tools and techniques. These are as follows:

(i) Day-to-day observation of classroom behaviour of children by the teacher.
(ii) Assessment of children's performance in specific subjects based on the Cumulative Record Card or school marks.
(iii) Opinion of parents about the child's progress and difficulties in learning various subjects, doing homework, his language difficulties, emotional problems, illness, injuries and physical defects and problems.
(iv) Measures of intellectual ability or IQ scores.
(v) Competence-based tests and diagnostic tests in various subjects.

However, if slow learners are to be helped in their learning difficulties, they must be identified early in schools, because prolonged learning difficulties may imply placement of such children in special schools which are very rare in India.

4. Educational Programmes for the Slow Learners

The slow learner is capable of achieving a moderate degree of academic success though with additional time and help. They are capable of being educated in the regular class with few adaptations. As adults, they are self-supporting, independent, and socially adjusted. If the needs of such children are not met, they experience failure and drop out prematurely from school. The difficulty is that most of these children are not diagnosed as slow learners until they attend school and begin to fail. This calls for early identification, diagnosis of their learning difficulties and proper instructional provisions for them.

Adolescent slow learners are usually benefited from the following plans:

Carefully Guided Instruction

Slow learners work best with a carefully designed, step by step technique, and additional time and help. Considerable repetition is usually necessary and the material should be adapted appropriately for the slow learner. Positive reinforcement technique should be used as much as possible. The following recommendations are useful for the teacher:

(i) The teacher needs to emphasize the concrete and the specific with regard to the problems and materials.

(ii) Instruction should be directed towards satisfying those needs that are more immediate and more easily recognised and identified.

(iii) Slow learners should be given more time, attention and guidance by the teacher until they reach the expected average standard.

(iv) Instruction should be less dependent on conventional printed materials.

(v) Out-of-school resources like the field trip should be used more frequently.

(vi) There is need for greater utilization of audio-visual aids.

(vii) Learning units should be organised around life's problems more than around academic subjects.

(viii) Teachers should avoid any kind of competition or comparison between normal or gifted students and slow learners.

(ix) All types of labelling such as 'stupid,' 'idiot,' the 'slow learner,' 'the dull,' 'the back bencher' should be avoided by the teacher as this may lower the child's self-concept, self-esteem and lead to greater frustration, anxiety, withdrawal and delinquent tendencies.

(x) Teachers should discover any specific skills slow learners may possess. If possible, let them demonstrate their skills for other students.

(xi) Teachers should be careful about the number of things taught and the abstractness of the material. Sheer numbers can overwhelm any one, especially the slow learners. The more abstract the material, the greater difficulty the slow learner will have with it.

Individualized Instruction

Slow learners can learn as well as fast learners if instruction is approached systematically and sensitively, if they are given extra time and if they are helped in their learning difficulties. This was the proposition maintained by Bloom (1965). Bruner, a cognitive psychologist, also held similar views. Any concept can be taught to any child if appropriate instructional methods and procedures are utilized. Individualized instruction is most useful in the education of slow learners.

In individualized instruction, the methods and materials of instruction are adjusted to the needs and abilities of individual learners. There are mainly three forms of individualised instruction, such as:

(i) Tutoring,

(ii) Individually Prescribed Instruction (IPI) and

(iii) Individually Guided Education (IGE).

Of these three forms, tutoring is a popular programme in schools and homes. The IPI and the IGE are new developments.

Tutoring

Tutoring is a face-to-face, one-to-one relationship or situation in which the tutor has the primary responsibility of helping a child in his learning difficulty. Tutoring may be also done in a small group consisting of four to five children, but the essence of the situation remains the same in a small group as in one-to-one situation: individual help, attention and time. Thus instruction that is individualised, whether in one-to-one situation or small group situation is called tutoring.

Usually teachers act as tutors, but able classmates, older students and adult volunteers can also be tutors. Older children can talk their language and can provide excellent models for them. Children teaching children is not a new idea; it is very popular in homes and schools.

Remedial Instruction

Slow learners are benefited mostly from remedial instruction. Remedial instruction for slow learners refers to two types of programmes:

(i) Eliminating ineffective habits and unwholesome attitudes and re-teaching skills which have been incorrectly learned. This refers to remediation of defects.

(ii) Teaching for the first time those habits, skills and attitudes which have never been learned but should have been and which are needed by such children. This refers to developmental teaching or developing increased competence.

Remedial programme involves taking a child where he is and from that point leading him to greater achievement. Remedial teaching is just good teaching concerned with two types of deficiencies — the presence of bad habits and the absence of good habits.

Remedial instruction requires proper diagnosis of their specific difficulties in various subjects and understanding their problems before actual instruction begins. In certain cases, slow learning is caused by factors other than low intellectual ability. For example, visual defects may cause reading difficulties;

emotional factors may cause general academic failure. In such cases, interview with parents and the classroom teacher or a simple medical examination may solve the problem.

Remedial instruction can be given by the regular teacher, full-time remedial teacher or visiting remedial teacher. In Scotland and England, a large number of schools are utilising the services of visiting remedial teacher who visits a number of schools in a single day and provides remedial instruction to the students who need it on a part-time basis. The remedial teacher is a specialist teacher who uses alternate learning materials, methods, audio-visual aids and workbooks in tutoring situation.

12

Identification of Disability

1. NEED FOR EARLY IDENTIFICATION

Disabled children, whether they are already studying in school or not attending school, should be identified as early as possible by parents in the home and later by teachers in the school. Early identification of disability is important for the following reasons:

(i) Early identification will lead to early diagnosis of children's needs and difficulties.

(ii) Early identification and diagnosis will help in obtaining appropriate aids and equipments for such children which will reduce their problems.

(iii) Early identification will lead to early intervention by parents and teachers.

(iv) Early identification and intervention will help in better exposure to education, better psycho-social adjustment and better achievement in the school.

(v) Early identification will help in the placement of the disabled child in the appropriate educational setting, timely care and services for the child by competent specialists.

(vi) Early identification will help in increasing their enrolment in the school, reduce the rate of drop out and increase the rate of retention of such children. Thus it will contribute to the attainment of goals of Sarva Shiksha Abhiyan.

(vii) Early identification will help in appropriate rehabilitation of disabled children.

2. METHODS OF DETECTION/IDENTIFICATION

There are different types of disabled children. Each type of disability has its specific symptoms. Thus the identification will vary depending upon the type of disability. Usually disabled children are identified by various methods — sophisticated equipments, electronic devices, testing and non-testing techniques. Identification of disabled children by means of sophisticated technology, electronic devices and testing techniques are not always feasible in our schools due to the following reasons:

(i) Specialists are not always available in all areas for conducting medical and psychological assessment of disabled children.

(ii) In most cases parents are not willing to take their children to city hospitals for medical and psychological assessment purpose.

(iii) Our teachers are not trained or competent to use testing techniques.

(iv) Identification and assessment of disability in private clinics is expensive.

In view of these difficulties teachers can make use of non-testing techniques which include:

(i) Day-to-day observation of children's progress and difficulties in school related subjects and activities.

(ii) Reports of parents about their children's problems and difficulties.

(iii) Reports of peers about a child's problems.

(iv) Identification checklists developed by NCERT, New Delhi for different types of disabilities.

In this chapter emphasis will be given on identification of disabled children based on check list. It must be noted here that identification of disabled children by non-testing techniques is always provisional. This must be followed by assessment by specialists as far as possible.

2.1 Identification of Visually Impaired Children

Identification of children who are born blind is almost always made by parents within the first year of life. Children with lesser visual impairments may not be singled out until elementary school when vision becomes important in the performance of school work.

One can take the help of a trained professional to identify the degree and nature of visual impairment. However, many children, especially those whose eyes may look normal by general appearance may not be identified for a long time. The teacher can identify children who might be having some sort of visual impairment with the help of the following check list developed by the NCERT, New Delhi. It must be remembered that no single behaviour signifies visual impairment. Existence of more than one behaviour should ring the alarm for referral to proper specialists.

Identification Check List for Visually Impaired:

Behaviour

(i) Rubs eyes excessively.
(ii) Covers one eye and titles the head forward.
(iii) Holds objects and books close to the eyes.
(iv) Asks other children when taking notes from the blackboard.
(v) Blinks more frequently.
(vi) Squints eyelids together.
(vii) Bumps into people or objects.
(viii) Unable to participate in games requiring distance vision.
(ix) Excessive sensitivity to light.

Appearance

(i) Crossed eyes.
(ii) Red-rimmed, encrusted or swollen eyelids.
(iii) Inflamed or watery eyes.
(iv) Recurring styes.

Complaints

(i) Eyes itch, burn or feel scratchy.

(ii) Cannot see well.

(iii) Dizziness, headaches, or nausea following close eye work.

(iv) Blurred or double vision.

After identification of visual impairment by the teacher, such cases should be referred to specialists for medical assessment.

2.2 Identification of Hearing Impaired Children

There are various methods employed for early identification of hearing impaired children. They fall mostly into one of the following categories:

(i) High risk registers.

(ii) Screening procedure.

(iii) Objective measurement.

In the high risk register, information on all risk factors that may cause hearing handicap in the child is collected with the help of a questionnaire from the mother. Children who present risk factors are followed up and studied by audiologists. This is a health-related identification procedure used by volunteers who are trained by audiologists. In the screening technique behavioral observation is used for observing the child's responses and reflexes to the given sounds at various frequencies, distance and loudness. Objective measurement is based on sophisticated technology which costs a lot of money.

The methods mentioned above are mostly used in developed countries. They are very expensive methods and are not used in India. Most of these methods are useful for identifying severely and profoundly hearing impaired children. They are not practically useful for parents and class room teachers. Parents, particularly the mothers, have a major role to play in observing the behaviour of infants and children at different periods and referring the suspected cases to the audiologists and ENT specialists for systematic observation. Thus, observation of infants' behaviour and response to different sounds at different period of their life is more useful and practicable than other methods.

A large number of mildly and moderately hearing impaired children do enter the regular schools. But they remain unidentified as having any degree of hearing impairment. Their problems go unnoticed and unattended and at times misunderstood as a result of which such children experience failure in academic and social situations. They drop-out from the school before completing elementary education. This has implications for regular teachers. Regular teachers can play a significant role in identifying hearing impaired children by observing their behavioural characteristics. The following check list developed by the NCERT, New Delhi will help teachers to identify hearing impaired children in the school.

Identification Check-list for the Hearing Impaired:

- Does the child ask for repetition of instruction?
- Does the child display restlessness and inattention?
- Does the child have any observable deformity of the ear?
- Does the child have a discharge from the ear?
- Does the child complain of pain in the ear frequently?
- Does the child turn his head frequently in order to hear better?
- Is the child unable to follow your instruction?
- Dose the child scratch his ear frequently?
- Does the child focus on the speaker's face while listening to understand speech?
- Does the child ask for help from fellow students in taking notes when the teacher explains verbally in the classroom?

If answer to four or five questions are marked 'yes' the teacher can suspect hearing impairment in the child. Such a child should be referred to the audiologist and ENT specialist for systematic investigation and assessment. If the assessment report indicates mild or moderate degree of hearing impairment the child can be integrated in the regular school without much difficulty. If the assessment report indicates severe or profound hearing loss the child should be placed in a special school for the deaf.

2.3 Identification of Mentally Retarded Children

(a) *Identification by Parents*: Every child passes through certain stages of development at particular time in his life. These are called milestones of development. Experienced women, mother and grandmothers in the family know what developments occurs at what ages. Knowledge of milestones of development helps in identifying children who have delayed development. Some of these common milestones of development and the approximate age of their attainment relevant to Indian situations are given in table 12.1.

TABLE 12.1

Normal Milestones of Development

Sl.No.	Milestone	Age
1.	Smiles at others	4 months
2.	Holds head erect	4 months
3.	Puts objects into mouth	4 months
4.	Rolls from back on to stomach	6 months
5.	Uses whole palm to grasp	7 months
6.	Makes sounds 'anna', 'ad dadda'	7 months
7.	Sits without support	8 months
8.	Responds to name	10 months
9.	Crawls	10 months
10.	Stands by holding on to an object	10 months
11.	Holds objects with thumb and index finger	10 months
12.	Stands without support	10 months
13.	Say 'amma', 'cakka', 'atta', meaningfully	15 months
14.	Walks without support	15 months

Sl.No.	Milestone	Age
15.	Tells own name	18 months
16.	Drinks by self from a glass	21 months
17.	Shows body parts when named	24 months
18.	Indicates toilet needs	24 months
19.	Speaks in small sentences	30 months
20.	Unbuttons clothes	36 months
21.	Gives meaningful verbal answer to simple questions	36 months
22.	Differentiates big and small	36 months
23.	Identifies boy or girl	36 months
24.	Can button clothes	40 months
25.	Combs hair	48 months

We have seen how a normal child develops. Early identification of mental retardation is made by seeing how much a child is delayed on the milestones of development. Identification of mental retardation is done by using certain questionionries or checklist called screening schedules.

Three screening schedules are given below. The first is for the children below 3 years of age. The second is for those between 3-6 years of age. The third is for those aged 7 years and above. In the description of normal milestones of development the mean age of attainment alone is given. However, the age ranges have to be taken into consideration while screening for developmental delays. Hence, the age range is given in the screening schedule 1.

Screening Schedule No. 1 (Below 3 years)

Sl.No.	Item	Normal age range	Milestone delay if not achieved by
1.	Responds to name/voice	1-3 months	4 months
2.	Smiles at others	1-4 months	6 months
3.	Holds head steady	2-6 months	6 months
4.	Sits without support	5-10 months	12 months

Sl.No.	Item	Normal age range	Milestone delay if not achieved by
5.	Stands without support	9-14 months	18 months
6.	Walks well	10-20 months	20 months
7.	Talks in 2-3 word sentences	16-30 months	3rd year
8.	Eats/drinks by self	2-3 year	4th year
9.	Tells his name	2-3 year	4th year
10.	Has toilet control	3-4 year	4th year
11.	Avoids simple hazards	3-4 year	4th year
12.	Has fits	Yes	No
13.	Has physical disability	Yes	No

If the child is found to be delayed in any one of the items given from 1-11 and if the child has fits or physical disability suspect mental retardation.

Screening Schedule No. 2 (3 to 6 years)

Observe the following:

1.	Compared with other children did the child have any serious delay in sitting, standing, or walking?	Yes/No
2.	Does the child appear to have difficulty in hearing?	Yes/No
3.	Does the child have difficulty in seeing?	Yes/No
4.	When you tell the child to do something, does he seem to have problems in understanding what you are saying?	Yes/No
5.	Does the child have weakness and/or stiffness in the limbs and/or difficulty in walking or moving his arms?	Yes/No
6.	Does the child sometimes have fits, become rigid, or lose consciousness?	Yes/No
7.	Does the child have difficulty in learning to do things like other children of his age?	Yes/No

8.	Is the child not able to speak at all? (cannot make himself understand in words/say any recognizable words).	Yes/No
9.	Is the child's speech in any way different from normal (not clear enough to be understood by people other than his immediate family?)	Yes/No
10.	Compared to other children of his age, does the child appear in any way backward, dull or slow?	Yes/No

If any one of the above items is answered 'Yes', suspect mental retardation.

Screening Schedule No. 3 (7 years and above)

1.	Compared with other children, did the child have any serious delay in sitting, standing or walking?	Yes/No
2.	Can the child not do things for himself like eating, dressing, bathing and grooming	Yes/No
3.	Does the child have difficulty in understanding when you say "do this or that"?	Yes/No
4.	Is the child's speech not clear?	Yes/No
5.	Does the child have difficulty in expressing without being asked what the child has seen/heard?	Yes/No
6.	Does the child have weakness and/or stiffness in the limbs and/or difficulty in walking or moving his arms?	Yes/No
7.	Does the child sometimes have fits, become rigid or lose consciousness?	Yes/No
8.	Compared to other children of his age, does the child appear in any way backward, dull or slow?	Yes/No

If any one of the above items is answered 'Yes' suspect mental retardation.

(b) *Identification by Teachers*: The screening schedules are very useful in identification of MR children by the parents. The teachers, psychologists and multi-rehabilitation workers can also identify MR children before they come to the primary school for education with the help of these schedules. But there are a large number of mildly and moderately retarded children who are already in school. If they remain unidentified and if their educational and other special needs are not met they will experience failure and dropout from the school. The teachers can identify MR children who are already in school by observing certain behavioural characteristics. The following identification checklist is recommended by the NCERT, New Delhi for identification of MR children who are already in school:

Identification Checklist of MR Children:

- Displays poor academic achievement constantly.
- Relies too much on presentation of concrete objects.
- Has a short attention span.
- Displays short term memory.
- Has a poor self-image.
- Lacks self-confidence.
- Has restricted communication.
- Seeks repetition and practice.
- Does not take any initiative in group activities.
- Often inattentive and distracted.
- Needs immediate reward.
- Displays fear of failure.
- Has poor muscular coordination.
- Faces difficulty in doing things for him.
- Has problem in understanding instructions.
- Is unable to sit in one place for more than a few minutes.
- Exhibits restless activities like tapping, pulling and so on.
- Have problems in speech.
- Is hyperactive.

After identifying a child with MR he should be referred to specially trained experts for medical and psychological assessment and diagnosis.

2.4 Identification of Learning Disabled Children

The LD children are usually identified by the following methods and techniques:

(i) Interview with children and their parents.

(ii) Observation by teachers.

(iii) Informal testing by teachers.

(iv) Formal testing by the assessment team.

Testing commonly used for identification purpose includes intelligence tests, achievement tests and diagnostic tests. The classroom teacher can identify such children by observing their behavioural characteristics consistently for a period of time. Observation by a team of teachers is more useful in identifying such children. The following checklist is recommended by NCERT, New Delhi for identification of LD children.

Identification Checklist for the LD Children:

- Has difficulty in telling the time, remembering the order of days, months and seasons and mathematical tables.
- Finds it difficult to organize his work and is often late in submitting his class work.
- Seems dull and slow in responding to others.
- Cannot correctly recall oral instruction when asked to repeat them.
- Does not seem to listen to or understand instruction given at home or in the classroom (asks for repetition).
- Shows excessive inconsistency in the quality of performance, from time to time, seems to be bright in many ways, but still does poorly in school.
- Gets easily distracted even by a slight disturbance.
- Confuses between left and right.
- Gets so excited that he cannot sit still in the classroom even for a short period.

- While reading, misses outlines or reads them twice.
- Finds difficulty in synthesizing a word after spelling its component letters:
- Example: says b/e/g but cannot say beg, or may say bed instead.
- Makes wild guesses at words whether they make sense or not (for example, 'huge', 'hurt', 'turned' for 'trainer').
- Reads word backwards (for example 'on' for 'no', 'saw' for 'was').
- Puts letters in the wrong order (reading 'felt' as 'left', 'act' as 'cat').
- Shortens words ('sunly' for 'suddenly', 'member' for 'remember').
- Misreads words which look similar ('help' for 'held', 'house' for 'horse').
- Has difficulty in recollecting words automatically and correct sentences.
- Misreads number ('6' as '9' '3' as '8') writes letters in the wrong order (time for 'item').
- Mirror writes (ram for mar).
- Reverses letter ('b' as 'd', 'p' as 'q').
- Mirror writes (6 as '9', 'q' as 'p').
- Omits letters ('limp' as 'lip', 'went' as 'wet').
- Adds letters ('want' as 'what', 'what' as whart').
- Does not write the appropriate letters when given the sound.
- Does not pick out letter of the alphabet when the name of the letter is called out.
- Does not match the letter when asked to.
- Difficulty in academic subjects. Sometimes the student is deficient in only one subject or a combination of subjects.

After identifying LD children by using the checklist mentioned above the teacher should see that such children are assessed properly by the experts. Such assessment may be medical and psychological. In most cases experts such as doctors and psychologists are not available for medical and psychological assessment of LD children. In rural areas particularly, trained professionals are not available. Functional assessment which is not a replacement of medical or psychological assessment indicates what a child can do and what he cannot do. Based on functional assessment the teacher can plan and provide specialized service and help in the school. The National Council of Education Research and Training, New Delhi has developed "Functional Assessment Guide" for use by teachers.

2.5 Identification of Orthopaedically Handicapped Children

Orthopaedic handicap involves a number of disorders — some are easily visible and some are internal and hence not visible from outside; some are simple and others are so severe that they draw our sympathy. Disorders which are external in nature can be easily identified by teachers. Disorder which is internal in nature can be better identified by orthopaedic specialists. However the following checklist can help teachers to identify children with orthopaedic handicap. If answer to three or four questions are found to be 'yes' the child is supposed to have orthopaedic handicap and he should be referred to the specialist doctor for medical assessment.

Identification Check List for OH Children:

- Is there any observable deformity in the child's legs/arms/palms/feet?
- Does the child walk awkwardly?
- Does the child feel pain in the joints?
- Does the child feel pain in his bones and muscles?
- Is there any loss of any part of his body?
- Is the child suffering from polio?
- Does the child feel pain in bending his knees?
- Is the child crippled?
- Is the child not able to walk or run some distance?
- Is the child's leg or hand abnormally short or weak?

2.6 Identification of Speech Handicapped Children

Speech handicapped children should be identified by specialist doctors and speech therapists. But parents and teachers can identity speech handicapped children on the basis of the following checklist:

Identification Checklist for Speech Handicap:

- Does the child stutter or stammer?
- Is the child dumb?
- Does the child have a cleft palate?
- Does the child's voice tremble?
- Does the child feel hesitant while speaking?
- Does the child stop in the middle of his speech?
- Does the pitch of his voice vary to a great extent?
- Is his pronunciation faulty?
- Is the child unable to express his feelings?
- Does the child use gestures and signs while communicating his feelings?
- Is the child's speech development delayed?

If answers to three or four questions are 'yes' speech handicap can be suspected.

13

Characteristics of the Disabled

There are various categories of disabled children. All categories of disabled children do not possess the same characteristics. In other words, the characteristics of disabled children are specific to the categories to which they belong. In this book characteristics of disabled children have been discussed category-wise.

1. CHARACTERISTICS OF VISUALLY IMPAIRED CHILDREN

Language Development

(i) Many studies show that the language development of the blind is unimpaired. The blind child is still able to hear language and may even be more motivated than the sighted child to use language because it is the major way in which he or she communicates with parents and peers.

(ii) Even though their language development is unimpaired it is different from the normal child's language. The language of the normal child is consistent with his sensory experiences. But the blind exhibits what is termed as verbalism or verbal unreality. Verbal unreality is defined as the blind individual's inappropriate reliance on words and phrases that are not consistent with his sensory experiences. Since the blind child explores his world primarily through the auditory, tactual and olfactory rather than the visual senses, it would seem that his language would reflect this fact. For example, most blind children perceive Indians as "red" or "brown" although they have no opportunity to see the colour of the skin. This is so because the blind are expected to appreciate things not as they themselves experience them, but as they are taught how others experience them. This verbalism is not inherent in the condition of blindness, rather it is taught to the individuals through the educational system.

Intellectual Ability

(i) The blind are not markedly lower in intelligence than the sighted. Children who have shown low IQ scores for a number of years in a sheltered environment suddenly make dramatic gains provided with adequate educational opportunities.

(ii) The conceptual or cognitive abilities of blind children are at least different if not inferior to those of sighted children. Deficiencies in conceptual development of blind children are due to lack of appropriate learning experiences.

(iii) They have difficulty in comprehending space. Not able to see distance, blind individuals are at a distinct disadvantage in appreciating spatial concepts by the use of other senses than vision. The blind sometimes develop an appreciation of space by noting the time it takes to walk various distances and through touch and kinesthesia. Audition provides clues to the direction and distance of objects which make sound but it gives no idea of the objects as such. Tactual and kinesthetic experiences require direct contact with or movement around objects. Thus distant objects such as the heavenly bodies, clouds and the horizon, as well as very large objects such as mountains and other geographical units or microscopic objects such as bacteria, cannot be perceived and must be conceived only by analogy and extrapolation from objects actually experienced.

(iv) The tactual sense is the primary way in which a variety of concepts are acquired by the blind child. There are two different kinds of tactual perception — synthetic touch and analytic touch. Synthetic touch refers to a person's tactual exploration of small objects which are small enough to be enveloped by one or both hands. Unfortunately most physical objects are too large for synthetic touch to be useful. Analytic touch involves the touching of various parts of an object and then mentally constructing these separate parts. Whereas the sighted person is able to perceive different objects or the parts of one object simultaneously, the blind person must perceive things successively. This necessity for perception in a successive manner restricts the blind child's ability to gain a conceptual understanding of his world.

(v) The visually impaired people develop an increased ability in attention because their reliance on other senses must be greater. They are very good at listening tasks. They score high on measures of creativity. Thus, even though they are greatly disadvantaged in terms of cognitive development they are able to compensate in many ways.

Mobility

Probably the most important ability for the successful adjustment of most visually impaired individuals is their mobility. Mobility refers to the skill of moving about in their environment. Mobility skills vary considerably in the visually impaired population. Some blind persons can move relatively easily through crowded city streets, some walk down a quiet street while some cannot move without a helper. The fact is that mobility would be better among those who have more residual vision than among those who have less. More significant is the fact that it is the motivation to become mobile that makes the difference.

Academic Achievement

Comparison of a visually impaired child's academic performance with that of a sighted child poses numerous problems. However, some gross generalizations can be made from the research that has been done.

(i) Both partially sighted and blind children are behind their sighted peers in terms of mental age.

(ii) The achievement of visually impaired children is not affected as greatly as is that of hearing impaired because hearing is evidently more important for school learning than is seeing.

Social and Work Adjustment

(i) Personality problems are not inherent in the condition of blindness. If maladjustment does occur in a blind individual, it is more than likely due to the fact that the society has treated him differently. In other words it is society's reaction to the blind person that determines his adjustment or lack of it.

(ii) The visually impaired children are not well accepted by their peers. The more severely impaired are better accepted than the less severely handicapped. This is because people's sympathy tends to increase with the severity of a disability or because the moderately handicapped actually exhibit behaviour that elicits more negative reactions from others.

(iii) It is not necessarily the fact that blind persons tend to be dependent and helpless. The dependency and helplessness of blind persons are a result of society's attitude towards and expectations from the blind.

2. CHARACTERISTICS OF HEARING IMPAIRED CHILDREN

Hearing loss can have profound consequences for some aspects of a person's behaviour and little or no effect on other characteristics. If you are asked to choose, "which would you rather be — blind or deaf?" most of your first reply will be to choose deafness, probably because of your reliance upon sight for mobility and because many of the beauties of nature are visual. In terms of functioning in language and academically-oriented society, however, the deaf child is at a much greater disadvantage. The psychological and behavioural characteristics of the hearing impaired children are given below:

(a) Language and Speech Development

(i) The ability to learn language and speech is the most severely affected area of development of the hearing impaired.

(ii) Without extensive training, the hearing impaired child will not develop normal language.

(iii) Earlier the hearing loss occurs, the more pronounced the language deficit will be.

(iv) The child who is born totally deaf will grow up mute unless special training is initiated (Carhart, 1970).

(v) The attitude that deafness automatically leads to an inability to speak is not scientifically based.

(vi) While profound hearing impairment is a great barrier to normal language development, there are very few deaf individuals who cannot be taught some use of language.

(vii) There are cases of children with hearing losses as great as 70 to 90 dB in the better ear who have nevertheless developed excellent speech (Fry, 1966).

(viii) Children who lose hearing after having been exposed to the experience of speech, even for as short period as one year, can be trained more easily in all language arts, even if formal training begins some years after they become deaf.

The deaf child demonstrates a particular pattern of babbling as an infant. The deaf infant enters the babbling stage at the same time as the normal infant, but soon abandons. This is because he or she:

- receives inadequate auditory feedback when he himself makes sounds;
- receives inadequate verbal reinforcement from adults;
- is unable to hear adequately an adult language model.

(b) Intellectual Ability

(i) Contrary to the popular notion, deaf children are found not necessarily slower in intellectual development than the normal children (Furth, 1961).

(ii) Thinking process of normal and deaf children is found to be similar (Furth, 1964, 1971).

(iii) The cognitive abilities of deaf children are essentially unimpaired except in those cases which involve language experience (Furth, 1961).

(iv) Deaf children who have not received adequate parental stimulation or educational instruction do perform less well than normal on intellectual tasks.

(v) Deaf children are retarded in intellectual tasks which require verbal skills. But in intellectual tasks which are primarily non-verbal in nature they are not found retarded.

(vi) Hearing impaired children get a higher score in non-verbal intelligence testing than in verbal intelligence testing.

(c) Academic Achievement

(i) Hearing impaired children are frequently handicapped in varying degree with regard to educational achievement.

(ii) They are particularly handicapped in reading which relies heavily upon language skills.

(iii) The gloomy picture of the academic progress of the hearing impaired, particularly the deaf, does not appear to be improving.

(iv) Only a small percentage of deaf individuals comprehend language well enough to read a college level text book (Furth, 1973).

(v) The gloomy picture of the academic achievement of deaf children is mainly due to the fact that academic atmosphere in school and colleges is predominantly verbal in nature and that the deaf children have deficiency in verbal skills.

(d) Social and Occupational Adjustment

(i) Social and personality characteristics of hearing impaired children are markedly different from the normal children.

(ii) Since social interaction depends upon communication and the hearing impaired children, particularly the deaf, have communication problems such children have problems of social adjustment.

(iii) Because of their communication problems and failure in social interaction such children live a world of isolation.

(iv) Such children have a strong desire for social interaction and social acceptance. But the hearing people do not accept them. This creates a sense of inferiority and frustration in the hearing impaired children.

(v) The hearing impaired children, thus, form a group of their own, an association of the deaf for their common interest and interaction.

(vi) A large majority of hearing impaired children are employed in jobs requiring manual work. Sometimes they are overqualified for a job in which they are placed. It is not clearly evident whether hearing impaired children can be successful in managerial and secretariat services, but the fact remains that employers do not prefer them for such jobs. But there is no reason why a hearing impaired person cannot succeed in occupations which do not demand verbal communication skills, particularly speaking ability.

(vii) The hearing impaired children are not different from the normal children in emotional adjustment. The same environmental factors which cause emotional disturbance in normal children also cause emotional disturbances in hearing impaired children.

All these characteristics are not necessarily to be found in all categories of hearing impaired children. The hearing impaired children may differ from each other in relation to these characteristics depending upon their degree of hearing loss and the age of onset of hearing loss.

(e) Other Characteristics

Some studies indicate that the hearing impaired child is inferior in intellectual ability, educational achievement and personal-social adjustment. These children score a relatively low score in IQ testing. In general their performance in academic subjects of the school is also poor. They face difficulty in personal-social adjustment. All these characteristics are mainly due to the fact that the hearing impaired child has not acquired the basic language and speech patterns which are required in intellectual functioning, academic success and social adjustments. This is particularly true in case of severely and profoundly impaired, congenitally deaf, and pre-lingually deaf and children with sensory neural deafness. Our experience shows that the mildly and moderately hearing-impaired children, children who had some language experience before they become deaf and children with conductive loss of hearing do better in IQ testing, educational achievements and social adjustment. They are immensely benefited from the use of hearing aid, auditory training and integrated education programmes, provided they are detected early and corrective measures are applied as early as possible.

3. CHARACTERISTICS OF MENTALLY RETARDED CHILDREN

What are the mentally retarded people like? The mentally retarded people have many things in common with the normal people. But there are also characteristics which are different. The characteristics of MR children are mentioned differently in different literature by various authorities. Some describe the characteristics which are generally noticed in MR children and then go on to say that all MR children may not display all the characteristics. Their argument is that there is a great deal of variability in the behaviour of the retarded and each MR child must be considered as a unique and separate person. Some authorities describe the characteristics according to the degree of disability and others in terms of their educability. From whatever angle one may consider, the characteristics of MR children are as follows:

(1) General Characteristics of MR Children

(i) *Slow reaction*: They respond slowly to what others say and to what happens in their surroundings. Sometimes they do not respond at all.

(ii) *Absence of clarity*: They cannot express clearly their thoughts, needs and feelings.

(iii) *Inability to learn fast:* They cannot learn anything new and different as easily as others. They are slow in learning.

(iv) *Inability to understand quickly:* They cannot understand easily what they see, hear, touch, smell or taste.

(v) *Inability to decide:* They can not take even small

decisions. They do not know what to do, say and so on.

(vi) *Lack of concentration:* Some mentally retarded children cannot give continuous attention to one person or one activity. Some of them have difficulty in changing from one activity to another.

(vii) *Short temper:* Some find it difficult to control their feelings. They may throw things all over, injure themselves or others.

(viii) *Inability to remember:* Some can remember only for a short time what they are told. Sometimes they do not remember at all.

(ix) *Lack of coordination:* Some have difficulty in sucking, chewing or eating, use of hands or moving from place to place.

(x) *Delay in development:* The mentally retarded children have delayed development.

(2) Specific Characteristics of EMR, TMR and CMR Children

Educable Mentally Retarded (EMR). The EMR children have IQ 50 to 75. They have normal appearance and remain unidentified until late teens. They function at an intellectual level generally limited to learning the most basic school subjects or skills such as reading, spelling, writing and numerical calculation. They are expected to learn up to the seventh standard. They can communicate effectively in everyday conversation; enjoy friendship and group and social activities. They can hold skilled or semi-skilled jobs. But at times they may need assistance in doing their job. They can be educated in regular classrooms.

Trainable Mentally Retarded (TMR). The TMR children have IQ 25 to 50. They are expected to have physical or sensory impairments and many tend to look different in terms of facial features and physical characteristics. They function at a level where formal academic learning is quite limited. They can learn to feed, toilet and dress self adequately. They can carry in rudimentary conversation, and do simple household work. But they need training in self care activities, language development and rudimentary academic skills. They are usually placed in special classes or special schools.

Custodial Mentally Retarded (CMR). The CMR children have IQ below 25. They are so much retarded in intellectual functioning and adaptive behaviour that they remain totally dependent on others for their existence. It is because of their severe retardation that they are institutionalized early in life. Their speech and toilet habits remain at a primitive level. Behaviour modification and environmental stimulation techniques are usually recommended for their training.

(3) Specific Characteristics of Mild, Moderate, Severe and Profound Retardation

(Please see table 3.4 in Chapter-3)

4. CHARACTERISTICS OF LEARNING DISABILITY CHILDREN

The LD children constitute a heterogeneous group. Some LD children have reading problems and some others have writing problems. Some LD children have problems of comprehension whereas others may have problems in telling the time, locating a place on the map. Thus, it is difficult to mention the characteristics which are noticed in all LD children. The most frequently mentioned characteristics of LD children include the following:

(i) *Ability level:* The ability level of LD children varies from near average to average to above average.

(ii) *Activity level:* The LD children may be either hyperactive or hypoactive. If they are hyperactive they show the following behaviours — constant motor activity, restless, tapping of finger or foot, jumping out of seat, skipping from task to task, etc. If they are hypoactive they fail to react or seem to do everything in slow motion.

(iii) *Attention problems:* The LD children have short attention span; they are easily distractible; they are unable to concentrate on any task for a very long time. They often perseverate. Their attention becomes fixed upon a single task which is repeated over and over; this may be motor or verbal.

(iv) *Motor problems:* The LD children are generally clumsy or awkward with poor, fine and gross motor coordination. They demonstrate poor tactile discrimination, excessive need to touch, poor writing and drawing performance.

(v) *Visual perceptual problems:* The LD children are unable to distinguish between stimuli (visual discrimination): they are unable to perceive a figure against a background (visual figure-ground). They are unable to fill in missing parts when only part of a word or object is seen (visual closure); they are also unable to remember and revisualise images or sequences very well (visual memory).

(vi) *Auditory perceptual problems:* The LD children are unable to distinguish between sounds (auditory discrimination): they are unable to obtain meaning from the spoken word and/or environmental sounds (auditory comprehension). They are unable to attend to important auditory stimuli by pushing all other auditory stimuli into the background (auditory figure-ground). They are unable to fill in missing sounds when only parts of the word are heard (auditory closure); they are also unable to remember auditory stimuli or sequences very well (auditory memory).

(vii) *Language problems:* The LD children demonstrate delayed or slow development of speech articulation, and an inability to organize words to form phrases, clauses, or sentences.

(viii) *Social emotional behaviour problems:* The LD children are impulsive in nature. They fail to think about consequences of their behaviour. At times they exhibit explosive behaviour. They display rage reactions or throw tantrums when crossed. They lack social competence. Their social competence is often below the average for their age and ability. They are unable to adjust to changes. They exhibit rapid mood variation, even from hour to hour.

(ix) *Orientation problems:* The LD children possess poorly

developed concept of space, and a distorted body image. They have difficulty in judging distance and size and in discriminating figure from ground, parts from the whole and left from right. They are disoriented in time and experience trouble relating to concepts like before and after, now and then, and today and tomorrow.

(x) *Work habits:* The LD children organize work poorly. They work slowly and frequently, confuse directions or rush through work carelessly.

(xi) *Academic disabilities:* The LD children have problems in reading, arithmetic, writing, spelling, telling time and even locating places on the map.

In general LD children posses these characteristics. But not all LD children demonstrate these characteristics. Some LD children may have one or more such characteristics.

14

Functional Limitations due to Disabilities — Their Educational Implications

INTRODUCTION

Disabled children are unique individuals. Their uniqueness may be noticed in one or more of the following dimensions: vision, hearing, movement, communication, intelligence and adaptive behaviour. Consequently these children are classified into the following types:

- Children with hearing impairment
- Children with visual impairment
- Children with mental retardation
- Children with learning disability
- Children with speech handicap
- Children with orthopaedic impairment
- Children with multiple handicap

Disability reflects the consequence of impairment in terms of functional performance and activity by the individual (WHO, 1976). In other words, due to impairment there is a reduction in functional ability of the individual. For example, due to the hole in the ear drum, the child is unable to hear normally. A visually impaired child cannot see properly because of faulty image formation. Depending, in part, on the duration of functional limitation disability may be short-term, long-term or permanent.

Just as impairment creates functional limitations, functional limitations handicap the individual. Functional limitations lead to disadvantages experienced by the individual or impose restrictions which affect his efficiency in day-to-day activities. The individual faces problems in interacting with his environment.

Even if the disabled individual has functional limitations due to his disability he has certain potentials which have significant implications for educational programmes and practices. Let us now discuss in more detail the functional limitations due to disability, the potentials of disabled individual and their educational implications.

1. Children with Hearing Impairment

The hearing impaired are those children who have a damaged hearing mechanism, and face difficulty in speech and language development. There is a loss of hearing. The degree of hearing loss is less in some children while it is more severe in others. Hearing handicapped children may be deaf or hard-of-hearing. The deaf are those who cannot hear even if spoken to very loudly. The hard-of-hearing are those children who have hearing loss but who can hear if spoken to very loudly and/or with a hearing aid.

"Deaf means a hearing impairment which is so severe that the child is impaired in processing linguistic information through hearing, with or without amplification, which adversely affects his educational performance. Hard-of-hearing means a hearing impairment, whether permanent or fluctuating, which adversely affects a child's educational performance but which is not included under the definition of deaf" (USA Public Law, 94-142).

The potentials and limitation of hearing impaired children for education in schools and colleges depend on the degree of hearing loss, age of onset of their deafness, and language experience acquired in the home. In fact, the ability to learn language, speech and reading is the most severely affected area of development of the hearing impaired. Earlier the hearing loss occurs the more pronounced will be the language deficit. But post-lingual deaf children can learn language much more easily than pre-lingual deaf children. Hearing handicapped children are found to be retarded in intellectual tasks which require verbal skills. Consequently their academic achievement is affected, because education in schools and colleges is predominantly verbal in nature. Moreover, these children experience difficulty in learning abstract concepts.

Even if hearing handicapped children have limitations in learning language and speech, mildly and moderately handicapped children and some severely handicapped children can learn excellent language (Fry, 1966), provided they are identified early, they are encouraged to use hearing aid regularly, they are given systematic auditory training, teachers present more visual cues in the teaching-learning process, and these children put in hard work under the encouraging guidance of parents and teachers. Mildly and moderately hearing impaired children have potential to learn and progress academically in integrated settings. Even severely hearing impaired children can also receive education in integrated settings after they learn the basic academic skills in special schools. There are instances of tremendous potential of hearing impaired who have acquired the highest qualification in their chosen subject or field and are highly placed in an occupation and in the society. A success story is given in Box-1.

Box-1

B.V.S. belonged to a Telgu family. He was the only son of his parents. While he was reading in class 1 of a regular school he was detected by the class teacher to have some problems in listening and following direction. He was turning his head towards his peers sitting close to him for taking notes. The class teacher informed his father about the child's problems. He was taken to the specialist doctor for medical assessment. He was identified to be moderately hearing handicapped in the left ear. His parents were initially disappointed but later took personal care for teaching language and speech to the child by a trained teacher. Since there was no special school for the deaf in his locality he was educated in the regular school.

With sincere efforts by his tutor and personal care by his parents he could learn language and speech and made satisfactory progress in the school and colleges. He did his M.A. in History as a private candidates, M.Ed, as a regular student and Ph.D. Later he joined the teaching profession as a Lecturer in Education.

2. Children with Visual Impairment

Depending on the degree of loss of vision these children have limitations in mobility, orientation about the environment, concept learning, comprehending space, and forming visual image. Learning in schools and colleges is mostly verbal in nature and requires language skills. Hence visually handicapped children have better potential for learning than hearing handicapped children because their language development remains unimpaired. Even if these children cannot learn through sight, they can learn through tactual perception — synthetic touch (for small objects) and analytic touch (for big objects). Even if they cannot be taught through visual cues they have enough potential to learn through Braille, large print materials and hearing. In fact the potentials of visually handicapped children are more fascinating than their limitations. A large number of visually handicapped students successfully complete university education. Most low vision and partially seeing children are able to receive education in integrated settings. In fact blind children after they complete their preparation in Braille reading and writing, mobility training and orientation training, can also be educated in regular schools along with their sighted peers. A success story of a girl is presented in Box-2.

Box-2

Meena was a child with low vision born to parents who had no other child except her. Meena's parents discovered her problem with sight when she was around 2 years old. This discovery made them extremely unhappy and they felt that their life has come to an end. To have a daughter and that also with visual impairment was a curse for them.

They took Meena to a number of doctors but with no respite. Meena's sight never improved and finally they left every things on fate. They admitted Meena to a special school for early intervention programme and after a few years admitted her to a regular school.

As Meena grew older she started becoming aware of her parents' disappointment. She decided to do a lot of hard work so that she could become independent and some how bring happiness in the lives of her parents. In school, the teacher never bothered to check Meena's copy nor had any expectations from her. Meena went to the special school after her regular school hours and put herself both body and soul in her studies. Her hard work brought fruit and she came second in her class.

Meena's parents were thrilled with Meena's success. On the other hand, when Meena's teacher saw her report card she only had a few words for her. These are:

"*How can you do so well? You must have cheated*"

3. Children with Mental Retardation

Mentally retarded children are those children who have a lower level of intellectual functioning and have problems in social adaptability. Usually a school-age child who does poorly in academic work is considered mentally retarded. But this is not fair. Poor performance in academic work is not necessarily due to mental retardation. A child will be considered mentally retarded only if he possesses low level of intelligence and demonstrates deficits in adaptive behaviour, the first two criteria being noticed during the period from birth to eighteenth year. There are different degrees of mental retardation. The potentials and limitations of different categories of mentally retarded children are given in table 3.4 in Chapter 3.

A success story of a mentally retarded child cited by Brolin and Kokaska (1979) is given in Box-3.

Box-3

In 1958, a four-year-old boy was taken to the University Hospital at Ann Arbor for neurological examination. After many hours of examination, tests, X-rays, and waiting, a verdict and sentence was handed down by the University doctors. The parents were informed that their son was mentally handicapped and the best place for him was in an institution for mentally handicapped. "Your son, at best, may some day be able to sell papers on a street corner," the doctors informed the stunned couple. But the parents placed the child in a local school.

The boy was loved and cared for not only at home, but also at school. Sure there was hard and rough times. It is not easy competing with other kids. But the love and patience of parents and teachers, particularly the efforts of devoted teachers, were there for nineteen long years. Neither he became an A student, nor a drop-out, but he could complete his high school education.

Source: Brolin, D.E., and Kokaska, C.J. *Career Education for Handicapped Children and Youth* (3rd ed.), Columbus Oh: Charles E. Merrill Publishing Co., 1979, 86.

4. Children with Learning Disability

Learning disability may be mild, moderate, or severe. It may manifest in reading disability, writing disability, problems in comprehension and communicating in speech and writing and numerical disability. These children show frequently certain disorders, such as perceptual disorders, attention disorders, difficulty in processing information, difficulties in memory, oral language disorder and an imperfect ability to listen, speak, read, write and do mathematical calculations. In spite of these limitations they possess average and above average intelligence. Hence they have enough potential to learn. In fact, a large number of learning disabled children are already in the regular schools who remain unidentified. If these children are identified early, if their problems are understood properly and if they are exposed to tutoring by competent teachers, most of them can rise to a height in commensurate with their ability.

5. Children with Speech Handicap

Speech handicap means a communication disorder which adversely affects a child's educational performance. Because of speech defects these children have reading problems. (Eisenson and Ogilivie, 1977). As problems of articulation increase, reading skills decrease among the first graders (Weaver, Furbee and Everhart, 1960). Because children with speech defects make errors in pronunciation or have poor rate and rhythm in their oral reading, they may not comprehend or interpret correctly what they have read. Because of anxiety such children avoid all forms of oral expression. But early intervention by a speech therapist can bring significant improvements in their speech. They are educable in integrated settings. They can perform all tasks and participate in all activities in the school successfully excepting those involving speech.

6. Children with Orthopaedic Handicap

Orthopaedically handicapped children constitute a heterogeneous group having different types of orthopaedic handicap and neuro-muscular disorder. Depending upon their specific handicap these children have limitations in activities such as running, climbing, jumping, walking, lifting loads, etc. They may have problems with use of bones, muscles and joints. But these children do not have problems in learning school-related subjects. They are educable in regular schools with necessary aids and equipments. In fact a large number of orthopaedically impaired children are already studying in regular schools. Most of them successfully compete university education and are well-placed in jobs, politics and in the society. A success story is given in Box-4.

Box-4

Sunita, a beautiful girl, was born normal. To her ill luck, she suffered from polio at early age. Probably because of ignorance of her parents she was not treated by specialist doctors for her disease. Consequently both her legs were affected. She was advised to use crutches.

With love and post-polio care by her parents, her own superior intelligence, dedication, hard work and sincerity in studies she grew to be a bright student. Like any other non-disabled student she had her dreams to receive higher education and live an independent life in future. All this helped her to complete postgraduate education and later research work leading to Ph.D. She is now well placed in a University Department.

7. Role of the Teacher

Disability creates functional limitations and imposes restrictions to make progress in the school. That does not imply that disabled children will not be able to receive education. In fact education is the basic right of every child whether he is abled or disabled. Society must grant this right to every child. The teacher has important role to play in this direction.

(i) The school and its teachers must ensure that disabled children are not denied the opportunity of receiving education in the inclusive school of his neighbourhood. An inclusive school is a school which welcomes every child, where everyone belongs, where every one supports and is supported by others. In fact the latest trend is to educate disabled children irrespective of their degree of disability in the inclusive school of his neighbourhood with necessary support services for teachers and students.

(ii) It is not enough for teachers to enroll disabled children in the regular school. Teachers must accept disabled children as equal members of the school community. They must show positive attitude towards disabled children. Research has indicated that the greatest barriers to inclusion of disabled children in the regular school are non-acceptance and negative attitude of teachers (Dash, Neena, 2005).

(iii) Teachers must avoid labeling disabled children as retarded, deaf, lame, handicapped, crippled, etc. Labeling is not a health practice for a number of reasons:

- Labels usually focus on a child's negative aspects. Once a child is labeled, teachers tend to think about the child only in terms of his inadequacies or defects.
- Labels lead to low expectations from teachers. Research in the field of psychology has proved that teachers' expectations are reflected in children's performances.
- Once a child is labeled, teachers tend to explain the child's poor performance only in terms of his disability and not in terms of instructional failure.
- A labeled child develops a poor self-concept.
- Labels may lead to rejection by the peers.
- Labels create a sense of helplessness, inferiority and stigmatization (Dash, M., 2004).

(iv) Teachers must ensure that disabled children enrolled in the school are provided quality education. Quality education depends upon a number of factors such as teacher-student ratio, interaction between the teacher and the disabled child, interaction between children with disabilities and children without disabilities, availability of appropriate learning materials, continuous evaluation and remedial instruction for disabled children, and adoption of suitable teaching methods, etc.

(v) Teachers must take measure so that disabled children enrolled in the school stay in and complete primary education. Some of these measures are:

- Teachers must keep themselves abreast with new knowledge and skills relating to education of disabled children.
- Innovative teaching-learning strategies such as peer

tutoring, cooperative learning, individualized instruction, collaboration and consultation among teachers should be adopted by teachers.

- Teasing and bullying by peers should be discouraged by teachers.
- Appropriate teaching-learning materials should be procured or developed by teachers for different types of disabled children.
- Children with and without disabilities should be encouraged and guided to develop friendship which will reduce peer rejection.
- Parents should be advised and educated to take personal care of their disabled children on matters relating to regular attendance in the school, giving support for doing home assignments and making satisfactory progress in the school. Research by Fuller, *et. al.* (1999) has demonstrated that to achieve academically children must attend school regularly. A study in Malawi found that students with higher rates of attendance had grater learning gains, and lower rates of repetition (Miske, Dowd, *et. al.*, 1998).
- Teachers can play a role in helping parents to enhance the "home curriculum" and improve the quality of their involvement in their children's education (Reading, 2000).

Index